W9-BHY-491

101 SCIENCE EXPERIMENTS

101 SCIENCE

By Illa Podendorf

Illustrations by
Robert Borja

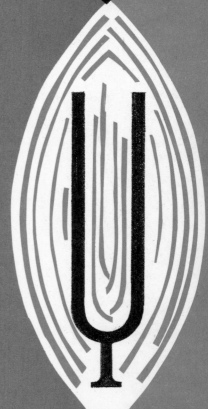

EXPERIMENTS

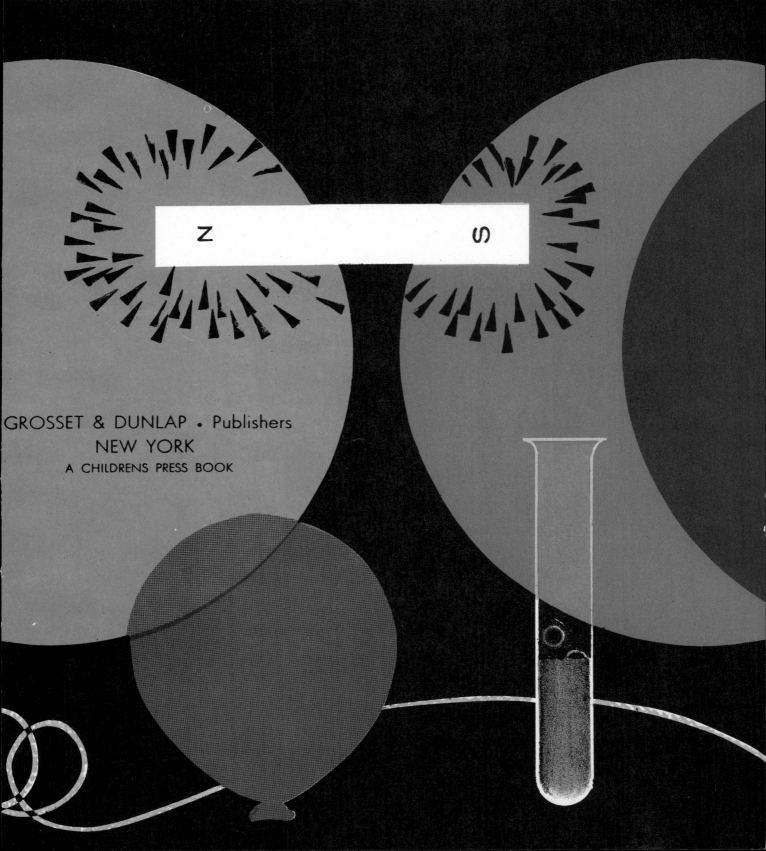

GROSSET & DUNLAP • Publishers
NEW YORK
A CHILDRENS PRESS BOOK

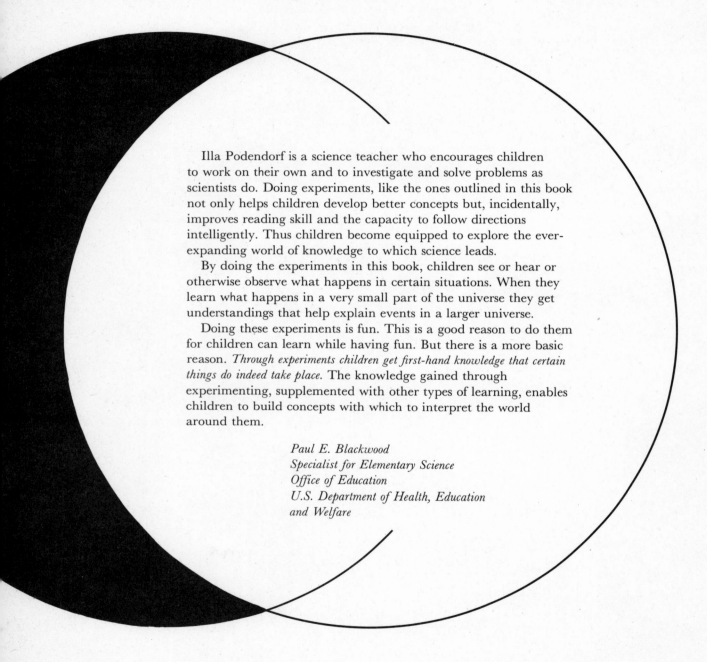

Illa Podendorf is a science teacher who encourages children
to work on their own and to investigate and solve problems as
scientists do. Doing experiments, like the ones outlined in this book
not only helps children develop better concepts but, incidentally,
improves reading skill and the capacity to follow directions
intelligently. Thus children become equipped to explore the ever-
expanding world of knowledge to which science leads.

By doing the experiments in this book, children see or hear or
otherwise observe what happens in certain situations. When they
learn what happens in a very small part of the universe they get
understandings that help explain events in a larger universe.

Doing these experiments is fun. This is a good reason to do them
for children can learn while having fun. But there is a more basic
reason. *Through experiments children get first-hand knowledge that certain
things do indeed take place.* The knowledge gained through
experimenting, supplemented with other types of learning, enables
children to build concepts with which to interpret the world
around them.

Paul E. Blackwood
Specialist for Elementary Science
Office of Education
U.S. Department of Health, Education
and Welfare

Library of Congress Catalog Card Number: 60-11157

This Edition Printed - 1962
Copyright, 1960, Childrens Press
Printed in the U.S.A.

CONTENTS

EXPERIMENTA

Most people like to experiment—to try something which they have never tried before—and see what happens.

Scientists do a great deal of experimenting. They experiment to find the right answers to questions and to find ways of making new things.

When scientists do an experiment, they look, listen, read and make records.

They are almost sure to plan an experiment if an experiment is the best way to find an answer to a question or to something which they wish to know.

Experiments are important, but scientists also use other ways of getting accurate information. They may watch growing plants or animals for a period of time and make careful records of what happens. They may collect and look at things. They may listen to different sounds. They read what other people have written about the subject that interests them.

Scientists may use several ways to find answers to their many questions.

When a scientist does an experiment, there are certain things which he is almost sure to do. He first decides what his question is—what it is that he wants to find out. Then he decides upon a plan for doing the experiment and gathers the materials which he will need.

As he thinks about the experiment, he will most likely form an opinion about what will happen. Then he will do the experiment. He will watch everything that happens and, if it is necessary, he will make a record of it. He will note whether his opinion was correct or not. He may need to repeat the experiment several times before he can be sure of the answer to his question.

It is easy to see that a scientist plans and carries on the experiment in a very careful way.

Some experiments need to be set up with a control. This means setting up the experiment in two parts. The parts will be just alike, as nearly as possible, with the exception of one thing. The way in which they are different has to do with the question which he is trying to answer. The eighth experiment with heat is an example of a controlled experiment.

In this book there are one hundred and one questions which we are almost sure to ask ourselves. For each question there is a suggestion for a way to find an answer to it.

Most of these suggestions are experiments.. They are experiments which scientists have done and ones which you might like to do.

When you do the experiments, you will want to work as scientists work. You must have the question clearly in mind. You must gather the materials together. You might then form an opinion about what you think will happen or what the answer to the question will be.

You must think over the plan for doing the experiment, and then follow the plan carefully. As you are doing the experiment watch, listen and think carefully to find out what happens in order to decide upon the answer to the question.

The answers to these questions may cause you to think of other questions. You may then plan other experiments for yourself. The answers to these questions and others which you may plan for yourself help you to understand the environment in which you live.

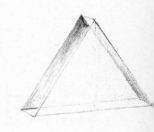

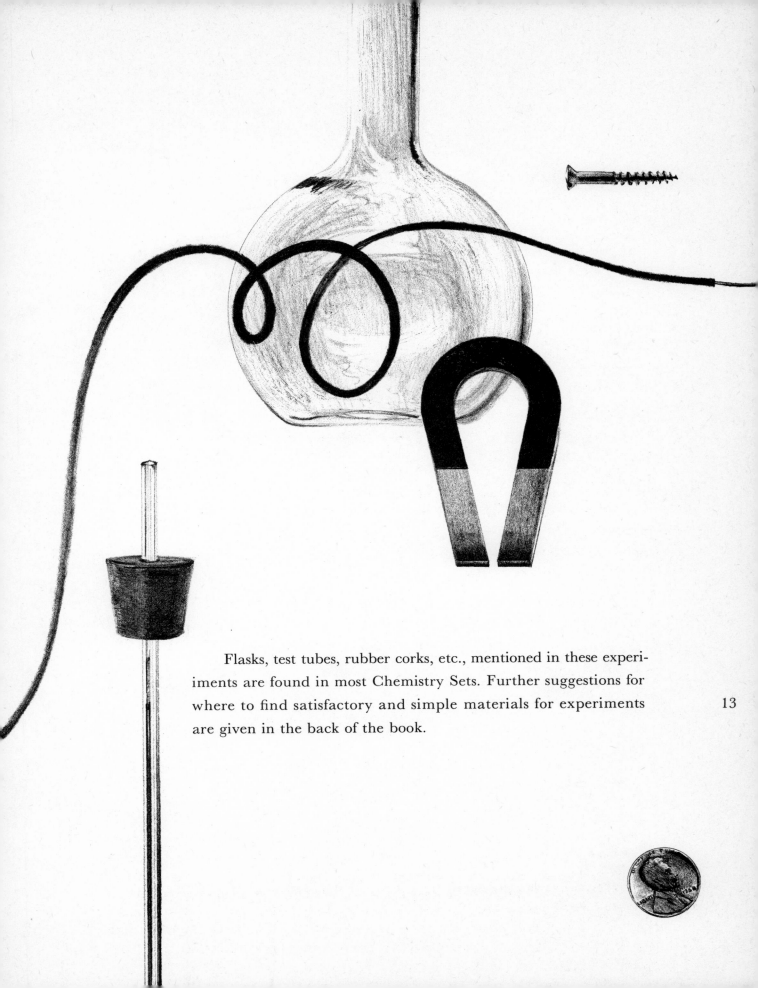

Flasks, test tubes, rubber corks, etc., mentioned in these experiments are found in most Chemistry Sets. Further suggestions for where to find satisfactory and simple materials for experiments are given in the back of the book.

13

14

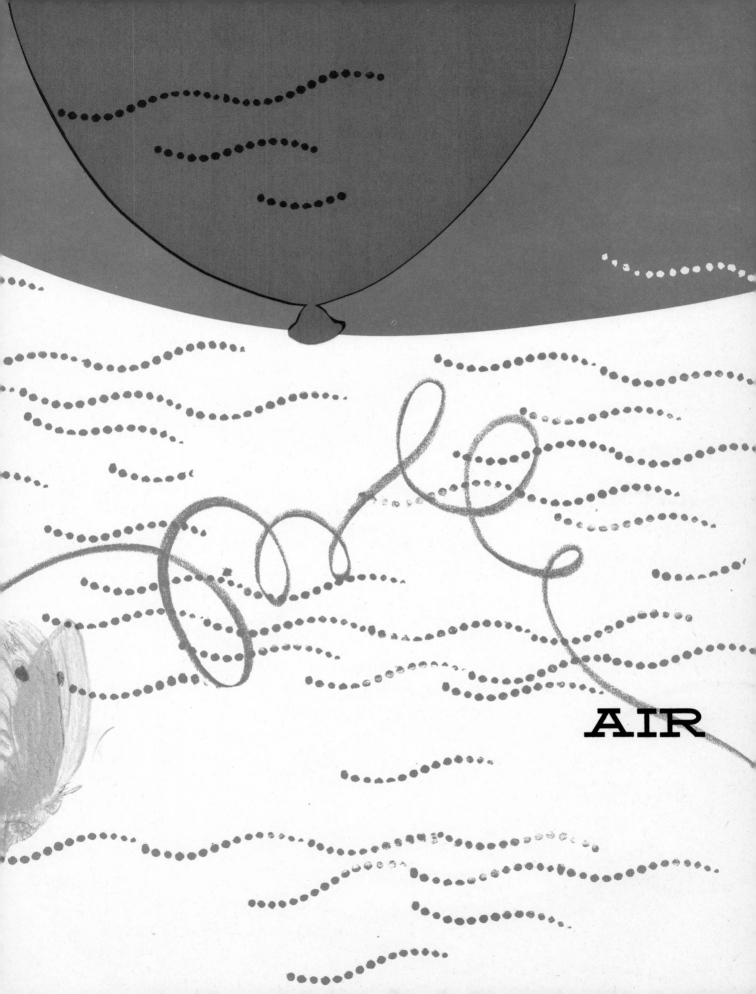

AIR

*1. Is this empty bottle really empty? You are sure to think it is.
Try this experiment and find out.*

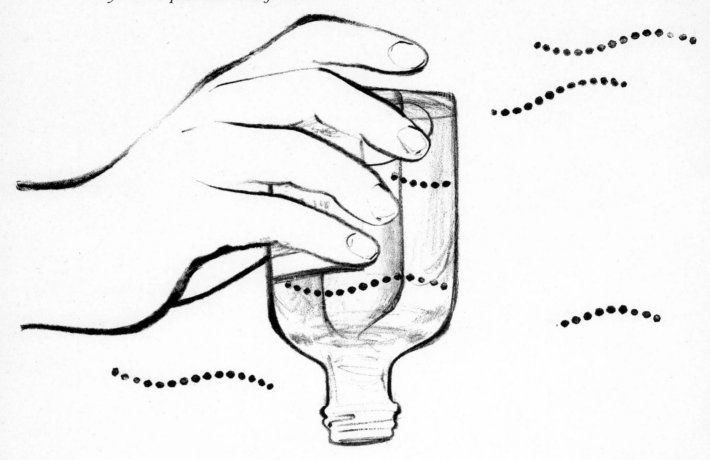

Turn the bottle upside down and lower it into the
pan of water.

Now tip the bottle a little to one side. Notice the
bubbles that come from the bottle and rise to the top of
the water. Try the experiment again and see whether the
same thing happens. The same thing does happen. The
 bubbles are bubbles of something. They are bubbles of air.
The bottle had air in it and the air had to be removed
before the water could go into it. Try other shaped bottles and see whether they can be made to bubble too.

16

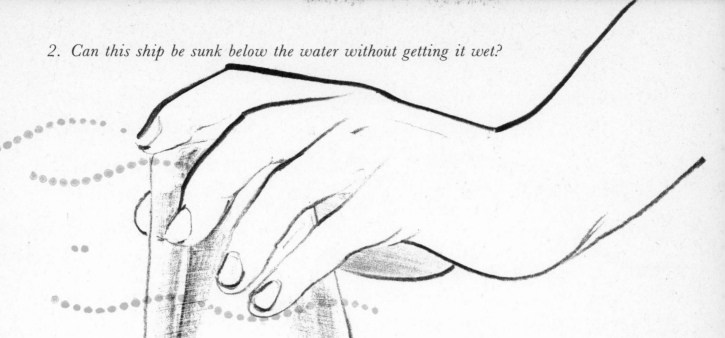

Make a ship by putting a sail on a cork as you see in the picture. Float the ship on the water in a jar or a deep pan. Be sure to keep it dry as you float it.

Turn a glass upside down over the ship and push it down. Raise the glass and examine the sail of the ship to see whether it is now wet. Try the experiment again to see whether the same thing happens. The sail stayed dry because there was air in the glass. The air kept the water away from the ship's sail.

This experiment and the first experiment show that air takes up space. Air is something—it is a material. If you remember this you will be able to understand the next experiment and explain the reason for what happens.

17

3. Into which of these flasks can water be poured easily?

Pour water into the one with the two-holed rubber stopper. Water runs into it evenly and without interference.

Pour water into the other one. The water runs slowly and with interference. Can you explain why this is so? You are right if you say the one with the second hole in the rubber stopper makes it possible for the air to escape as the water runs into it. The other one makes it difficult for the air to escape. This can be explained because air takes up space.

Could you think of something to do to the one with hiccups to make the water run into it evenly? You may say—loosen the cork. Try it and see if it works. It should.

4. Can this flask be made to blow bubbles?

Put the stopper which has a tube through it into the flask. Any bottle may be used. But the results are obtained with lightweight glass. Now put the end of the tube in water. Hold the ball of the flask in both hands for a few minutes. See what happens. See how many bubbles you are able to get.

Can you explain why the bubbles come out of the tube? You are right if you say it is because the air in the flask gets warm and needs more room. We say that air expands when it is heated. Now you have learned another important fact about air.

18

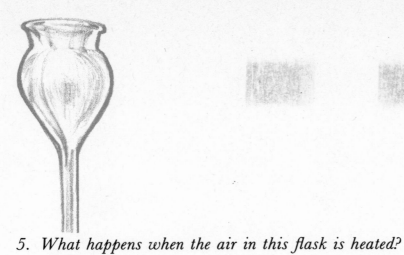

5. *What happens when the air in this flask is heated?*

Hold both your hands on the flask above the water line. Try to decide what you think will happen—in other words make a prediction. After several minutes decide whether your prediction was correct. What did happen? Did the water in the flask rise in the tube? Why do you think the water came up in the tube? You are right if you say it is because the air in the flask expanded and pushed the water up in the tube.

If you take your hands off and the air cools, the water in the tube will go down again. It goes down because the air in the flask contracts and takes up less room.

19

6. What happens when the air in this flask is heated? Make a prediction about what you think will happen.

Put a balloon on an empty flask.

Make your prediction before you read any further. Now hold the flask over an alcohol lamp and see what happens. The balloon is sure to blow up. It blows up because the air in the flask expands and takes up more room. You remembered an important idea about air if you made the right prediction.

20

7. *In this picture you see a balloon turned inside out in a flask. Do you wonder how this experiment was done? How did the balloon get into the flask?*

Put a small amount of water in the flask. Heat it until it boils. Now put the balloon over the mouth of the flask and let it cool. The balloon will slowly go down into the flask. The heat caused the air to expand and some of it go out of the flask. The heat caused the water to boil and some of it to change to steam. The steam pushed more of the air out of the flask. Now after the balloon was put on the mouth of the flask no more air could get in or out. When the water stopped boiling and began to cool the steam in the flask changed back to water. The air that was in the flask contracted when it cooled. Now there was room in the flask for more air. The only way the air could get in was for the balloon to go in, too. The balloon really was pushed in by the air on the outside of flask and balloon.

21

8. Does air really weigh something?

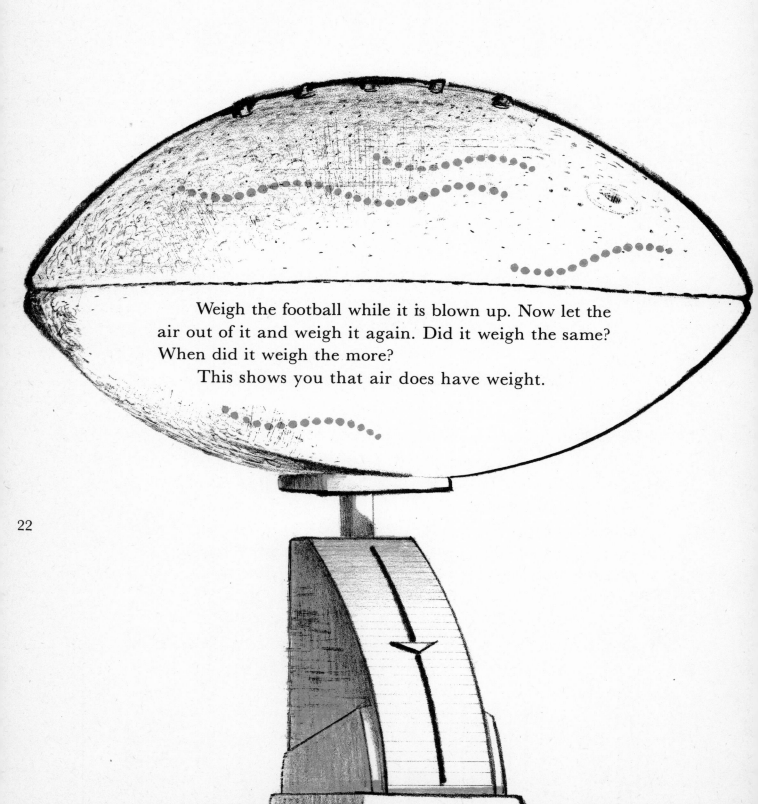

Weigh the football while it is blown up. Now let the air out of it and weigh it again. Did it weigh the same? When did it weigh the more?

This shows you that air does have weight.

22

9. *You are sure to know that air moves. Did you ever wonder why? Why does air move?*

Hold the pin wheel about 18 inches above a cold radiator. Does it turn? Hold it over a warm radiator. Does it turn? Hold the pin wheel about 18 inches above an electric plate which is not connected. Does it turn?

Hold the pin wheel about 18 inches over the electric plate and connect up the plate. Does the wheel turn? The heat causes the air to expand. When air expands it becomes lighter because the molecules move farther apart. Because the air which was not heated is heavier it moves down and pushes the warm air up.

10. What happens to a lighted candle when it is covered up?

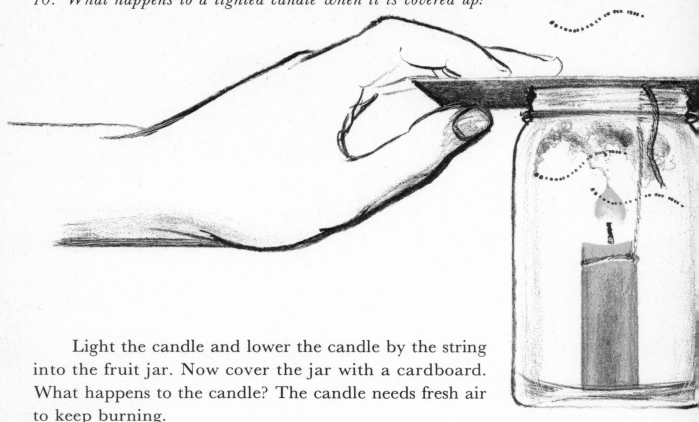

Light the candle and lower the candle by the string into the fruit jar. Now cover the jar with a cardboard. What happens to the candle? The candle needs fresh air to keep burning.

Here is another way to do this experiment.

Heat the wax on the end of the candle and stand it up in the dish. Now pour water around the candle. Turn the milk bottle over the lighted candle. The candle will soon go out and the water will rise around it. The water rises because the candle burned up part of the air and water came in to take its place. If you noticed bubbles escaping as you put the milk bottle down over the candle, they are bubbles of air. The heat from the candle caused the air to expand and some of it escaped in the bubbles.

24

11. Why do suction-cup darts stay on a target? Perhaps this experiment will help you understand the reason.

Remove the bulbs from a couple of medicine droppers. Squeeze them so that most of the air is forced out of them. Now put them, one at a time, on your arm. You can feel them hanging there. You remember that you pushed most of the air out of the bulbs. Now there is more air pushing on the outside of the bulbs than there is on the inside. It is the air pushing on the outside that holds them there.

It is the air on the outside of the darts that holds them there. Most of the air on the inside of the darts was forced out when the dart hit the target.

*12. Air pressure is very helpful to us. You could not drink through
a straw if it were not for air pressure. How can that be true?*

Put two straws in a glass of milk, or lemonade, or
coke—whatever you would like to drink. Place one of
the straws in your mouth and suck on it. When you suck
on it you are taking some of the air out of the straw.
Now the air on the outside of the straw pushes down on
the liquid and forces it up to take place of the air which
you took out of the straw. You will notice that there is
no liquid in the other straw. The liquid will come up in
it, too, if you take the air out of it.

Now you know that:

Air is a material—it takes up space.

Air expands when it is heated.

Air contracts when it is cooled.

Air weighs something.

Air pushes in all directions.

Air moves.

Fire needs air to burn.

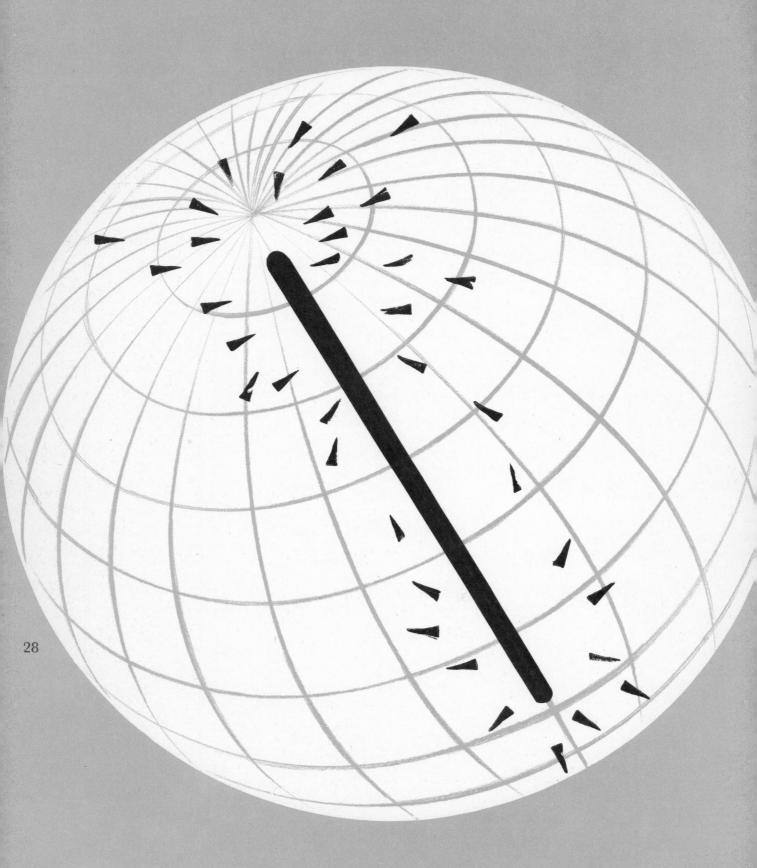

28

MAGNETS

1. Everyone knows magnets will pick up things. What kinds of things will a magnet pick up?

Make a collection of at least twenty small things such as paper clips, pins, rubber bands, matches, marbles, beads, etc. Try picking each of them up with the magnet. Put each thing which you can pick up with the magnet in one pile and put all the others into another pile.

Examine each pile carefully and decide what kinds of things magnets will pick up. You will doubtless decide that magnets pick up only things made of iron or steel. You will be right. There are a few other kinds of metals which magnets will pick up but they are not common ones.

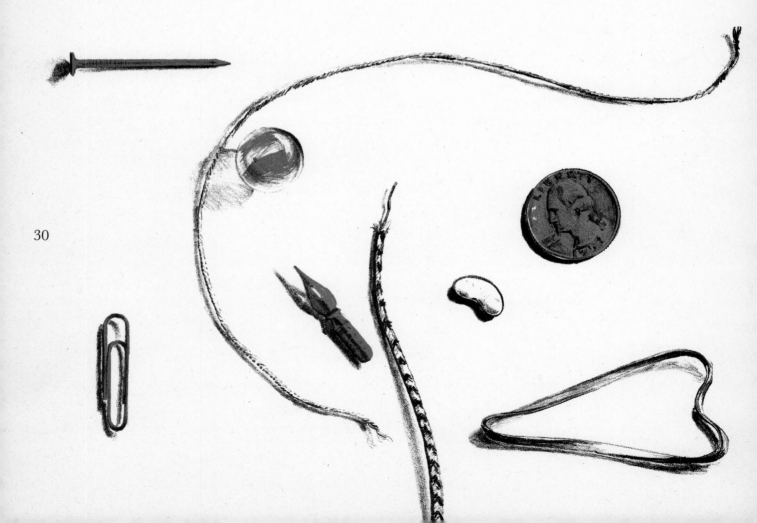

2. Are big magnets stronger than little magnets?

Collect several magnets of different sizes. Have ready a large pile of paper clips. Use two of the magnets, one larger than the other. Find out how many paper clips each of them will pick up. Do this over again with two other magnets. You will need to do this many times with different combinations of magnets—always one bigger than the other.

You are almost sure to have discovered that some of the smaller magnets are just as strong or stronger than the bigger ones. If you did not discover this you will need to try the experiment again with another collection of magnets.

The size of a magnet does not show how strong it is. It is the age and how well the magnet has been cared for that counts. This experiment shows us how important it is to do an experiment many times before we can be sure of a correct answer to a question.

31

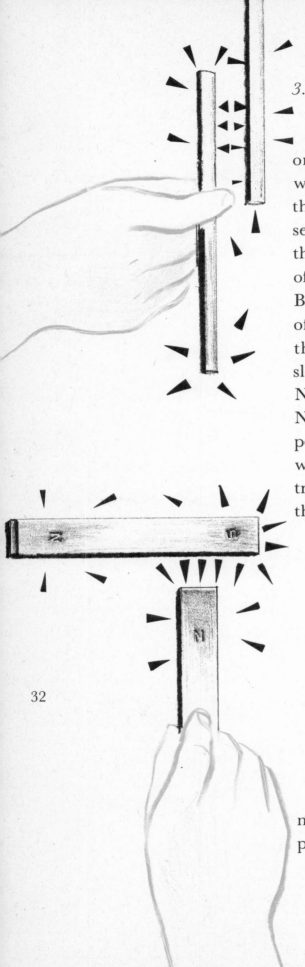

3. Will one magnet attract another magnet?

Use two pencil-shaped magnets. Lay one of them on the table. Bring the other slowly up beside it and see what happens. Do this several times. Now turn one of them around and do the experiment over again. Do this several times. Now use the bar magnets. You will notice that there is an *N* on one end and an *S* on the other end of each of them. Lay one of the bar magnets on the table. Bring slowly the S pole of the other magnet up to S pole of the magnet on the table. Notice what happens. Turn the magnet in your hand around and bring the N pole slowly up to the S pole of the magnet on the table. Notice what happens. Try bringing the S pole up to the N pole of the magnet on the table and notice what happens. Bring the N pole up to the N pole and again notice what happens. If you have another pair of bar magnets try this experiment with them, and see whether the same things happen.

You have probably come to the following conclusions:

An S pole will cling to an N pole.
An S pole will push away another S pole.
An N pole will cling to an S pole.
An N pole will push away another N pole.
You could say this in another way:
Poles which are alike repel each other.
Poles which are not alike attract each other.

You have really discovered the laws of poles of magnets. Perhaps you are wondering, do other magnets have poles?

4. Do round magnets have poles?

Hold the round magnet up so that it can swing freely. Bring one end of the bar magnet up to "one end" of the round magnet. Now turn the bar magnet around and bring it up to the same end of the round magnet. Have you decided that the round magnet has poles? You probably have, because one time the magnets attracted each other and the other time they did not. They repelled each other.

5. Can magnets be used as compasses?

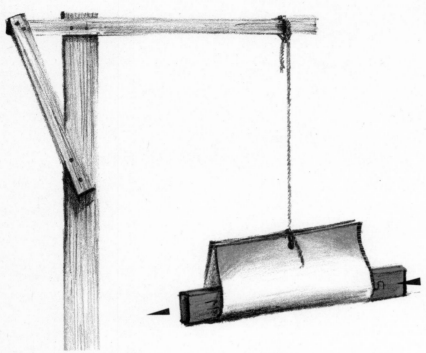

Make a standard or support for a bar magnet. It needs to be made from wood or from something which magnets will not attract. Make a hammock for the magnet by folding a piece of paper around it and tying the two ends of the paper to a string which hangs from the support. Now place the magnet in the hammock and let it swing freely.

After a few minutes it will come to rest. If you look carefully you will see that the North pole is pointing toward the north. The N pole gets its name because it points north. It should really be called the north-seeking pole. The S pole should be called the south-seeking pole.

A bar magnet could be used as a compass. If you had not known which direction was north you could have examined the magnet and then you would have known. The needle in a compass is really a magnet.

6. Can a magnet be made out of a steel needle?

Hold the needle in one hand. Take the magnet in the other hand and touch one end of the magnet to one end of the needle. Stroke the needle with the magnet. When the magnet reaches the other end of the needle it should be raised away from the needle and brought back to the starting end. The stroking should be continued fifty to seventy-five times—always stroking in one direction, and with one end of the magnet.

Now see whether your steel needle will pick up a pin. If it does you have made a magnet. You could make a compass out of your magnet. You could lay the needle on a cork and float the cork on water.

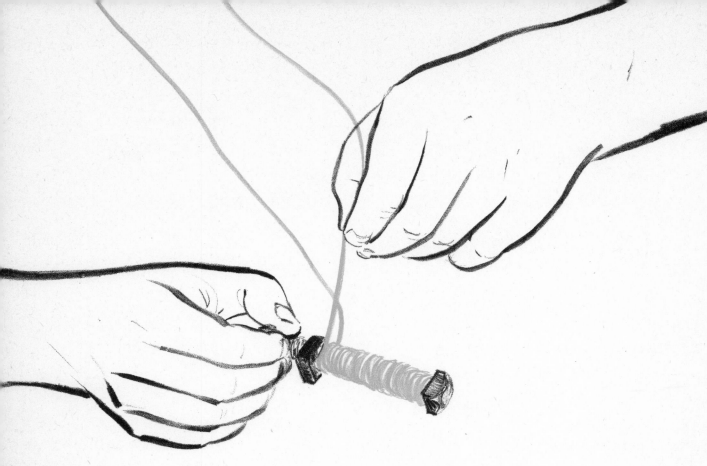

7. *How are electric magnets made to work?*

Find an iron stove bolt about two inches long. Be sure the bolt is iron because your electric magnet will not work if it is steel.

Measure off about 6 yards of cotton covered copper wire #24.

Wrap the iron bolt tightly with paper and tape the paper in place.

Start wrapping the wire on the bolt by beginning at the nut end. Leave about one foot of wire at the end so there will be some for connections.

When you have reached the other end of the bolt, turn it around and keep on wrapping. This will make a second layer of wire on the bolt. You may have enough wire to make a third layer. Leave about a foot of wire at this end too so that it can be used for connections.

Twist the two wires firmly together close to the bolt. Now you are ready to connect up your magnet.

Push the cotton back from the ends of the wire so that the copper shows. Twist one wire around one of the posts of a dry cell. Twist the other wire around the other post. Now see whether you can pick up paper clips with your electric magnet. You should be able to pick up several paper clips.

Now loosen one of the wires from the dry cell and see what happens to the paper clips. The paper clips should fall. This is why electric magnets are so useful— they are only magnets when there is electricity going through them. They can be made to pick up and drop loads.

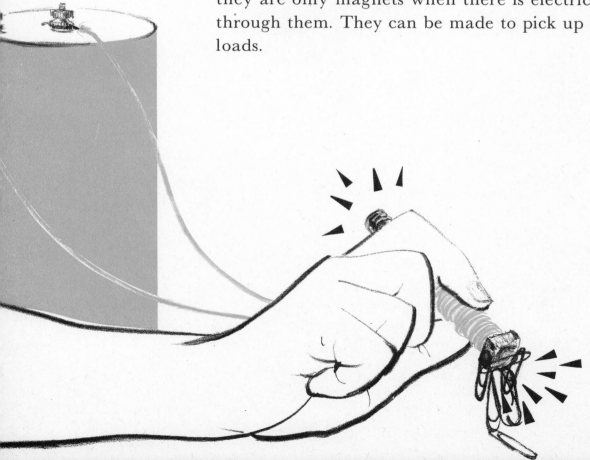

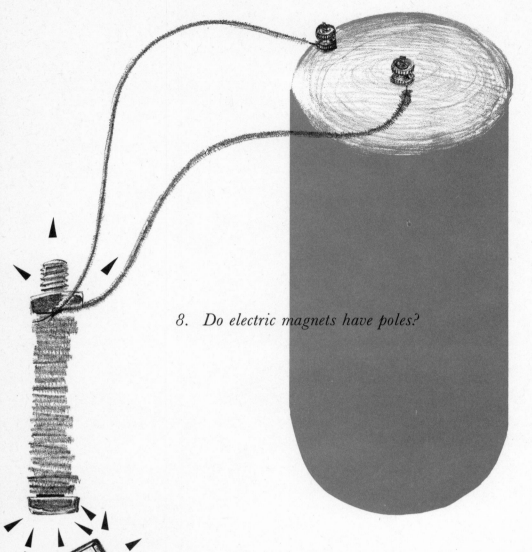

8. *Do electric magnets have poles?*

Connect up your electric magnet. Lay the electric magnet on a table. Slowly move one end of the bar magnet toward one end of the electric magnet. Notice what happens. Now turn the bar magnet around and hold the end of it toward the same end of the electric magnet. Notice what happens.

Do you have reason to think that the electric magnet has poles? You might try this same experiment on the other end of the electric magnet. Electric magnets do have poles—N and S poles.

9. *Can the poles of electric magnets be changed?*

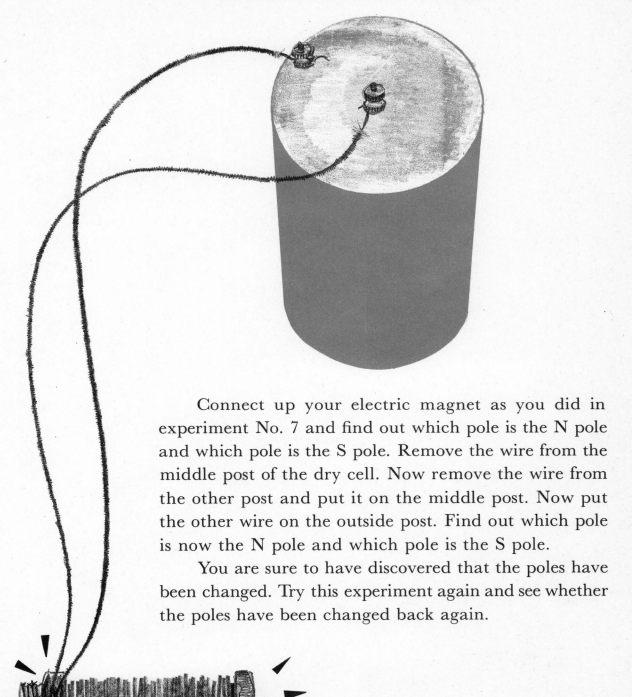

Connect up your electric magnet as you did in experiment No. 7 and find out which pole is the N pole and which pole is the S pole. Remove the wire from the middle post of the dry cell. Now remove the wire from the other post and put it on the middle post. Now put the other wire on the outside post. Find out which pole is now the N pole and which pole is the S pole.

You are sure to have discovered that the poles have been changed. Try this experiment again and see whether the poles have been changed back again.

39

Connect up your electric magnet as you have been doing. Test it to see how many paper clips it will pick up. Now remove the wire from the center post and put it on the center post of another dry cell. With another wire connect the center post of one dry cell to the outside post of the other dry cell.

Now find out how many paper clips the electric magnet will pick up. This is one way of making an electric magnet stronger.

40

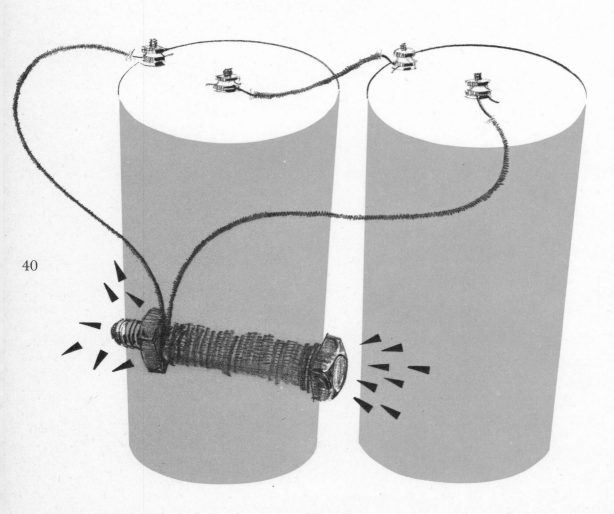

Now you know that:

Magnets will pick up things made of iron and steel.

The size of a magnet does not determine its strength.

Magnets attract other magnets according to laws of poles.

Different shaped magnets have poles.

Magnets can be used as compasses.

Magnets can be made.

Electric magnets work only when a current of electricity flows through them.

Electric magnets have poles.

An electric magnet can be made from an iron bolt and cotton-covered copper wire.

The poles of electric magnets can be changed.

An electric magnet can be made stronger.

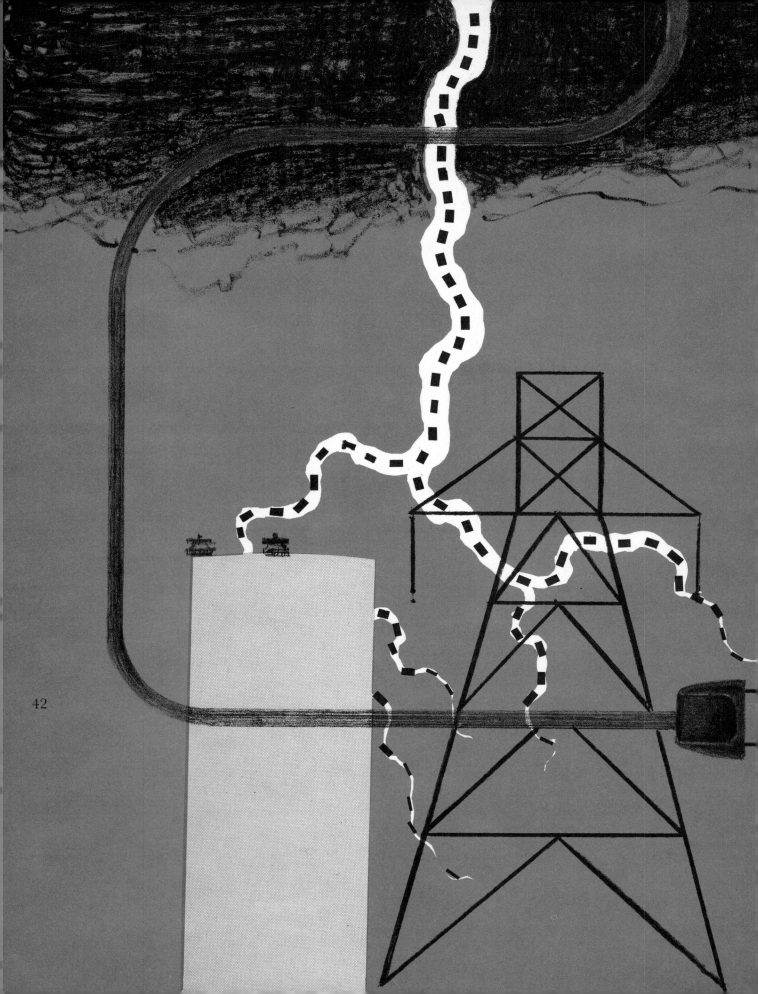

ELECTRICITY

1. How can the current in the electric magnet be turned off and on more easily?

Connect one wire of your electric magnet to the dry cell.

Connect another cotton covered copper wire to the other post of the dry cell.

Find a small block of wood about 2 inches long and 1 inch wide. Pound 2 small nails into the block of wood about 1½ inches apart. Now wrap the loose end of wire from the electric magnet around one nail and the other loose end of wire around the other nail. See whether your electric magnet will work.

It will not work because the electricity can not go from one nail to the other. This is a broken circuit.

We can make it a complete circuit by making a loop of wire which can be hooked from the copper wire on one nail to the copper wire on the other nail. You can use a copper strip if you wish. You have made a switch. Your electric magnet can be turned off and on. There are many kinds of switches. Some look like this.

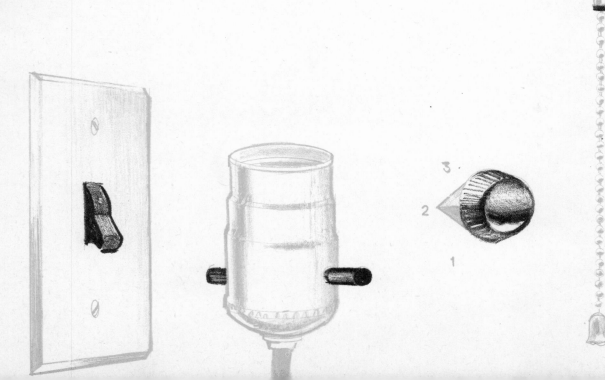

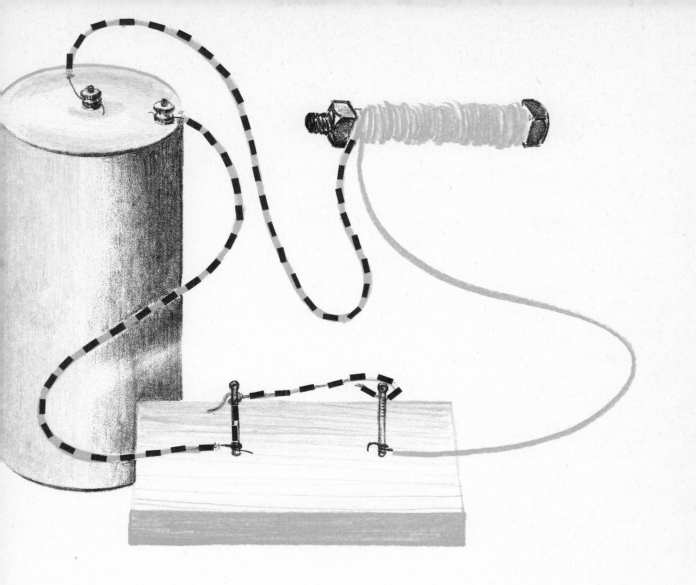

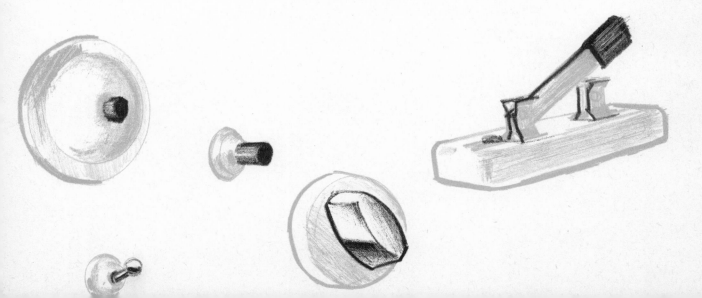

2. *How can a bell be connected with two dry cells so that it will ring?*

Use cotton covered copper wire. Connect two dry cells together. Be sure you connect a positive post and a negative post. This is important because electricity goes from the positive to the negative.

The positive post is in the middle and the negative post is on the outside.

Connect a wire to a switch and to one of the posts of one of the dry cells.

Connect a wire to the other post on the other dry cell.

Connect a wire to the other end of the switch. Now you are ready to connect the bell. You will notice there are two screws on the bell.

Connect one of the loose wires to one screw and the other to the other screw. Now see whether your bell will ring. Do you wonder why your bell rings? If you look carefully you will see an electric magnet in it. When the switch is on, the electric magnet pulls the clapper over so it hits the bell. This breaks the circuit and the clapper goes back. When it goes back the circuit is completed again and the clapper once more is pulled over to hit the bell. This happens so fast that the bell continues to ring as long as the switch is down.

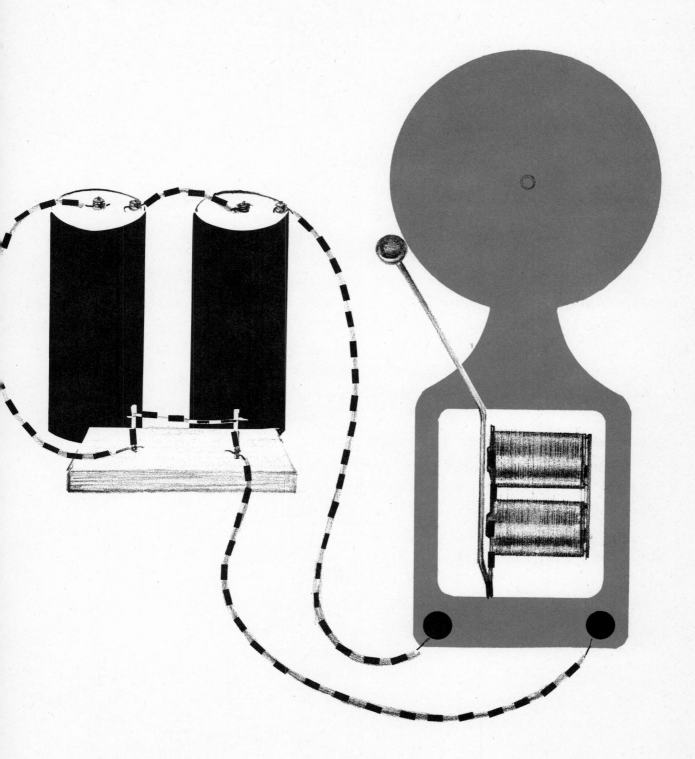

47

3. Why does a bell sometimes ring all the time?

Connect up the bell as you did in experiment 2 so that it will ring when the switch is down. Suppose you had a bit of wire left at the end when you connected it to one end of the switch and this wire accidentally touched the other side of the switch. Fix it this way and see what happens. Now the bell rings whether the switch is down or not. In fact the wire acts just like the arm of the switch.

48

There are other things which may cause the bell to ring all the time. Some insulation may be off of the wire in two places and these wires may accidentally touch each other. Electricity goes the shortest path and sometimes the shortest path is not the way we want it to go. We call this a short. All wiring must be done carefully and only good wire used. Shorts cause a great deal of heat and may cause a fire.

*4. Will other things besides copper wire conduct electricity suffi-
ciently to light a lamp bulb?*

Connect two dry cells, light bulb and switch. Open the switch. One at a time substitute the following materials for the copper strip or knife of the switch—brass curtain rod, iron nail, match, string, and strip of aluminum foil.

Which ones conducted electricty? How did you know they conducted the electricity? Of course the light bulb lighted only when the electricity was conducted. You probably noticed all of the metals conducted and the non-metals did not. You might try other things such as scissors, rubber bands, screw driver and see whether they conduct.

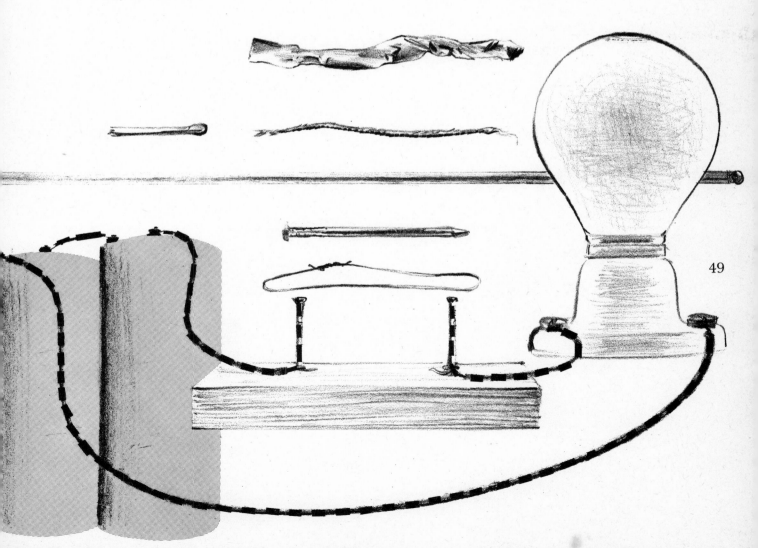

49

5. *What good is a fuse? This experiment will help you understand how a fuse works. You can see it work.*

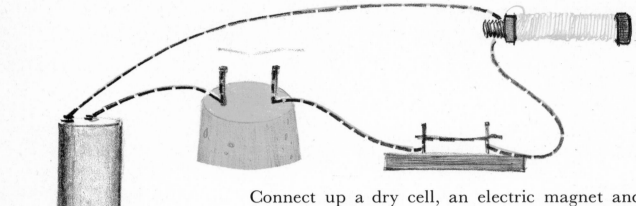

Connect up a dry cell, an electric magnet and a switch. Now cut the wire between the switch and dry cell and you will have a broken circuit even when the switch is closed.

Use a cork to represent a fuse. Place two small nails about ½ inch apart in the cork. Wrap one of the loose wires around one nail and the other loose wire around the other. Now you place a very thin piece of iron picture wire from one nail to another allowing it to touch the copper wire which is around the nails. The picture wire must be thinner than the copper wire. Close the switch and see whether the electric magnet works.

Make the magnet stronger by placing another dry cell in the circuit and see whether it works. You may decide to place a third dry cell in the circuit and make the electric magnet even stronger.

Something is almost sure to have happened to the wire in the fuse by now. It may have burned out when you added the second dry cell, or it may have burned out when you added the third. It is easy to see that a fuse is very helpful. The wire in it will melt and break the current. This may prevent the rest of the wire from getting too hot and causing a fire.

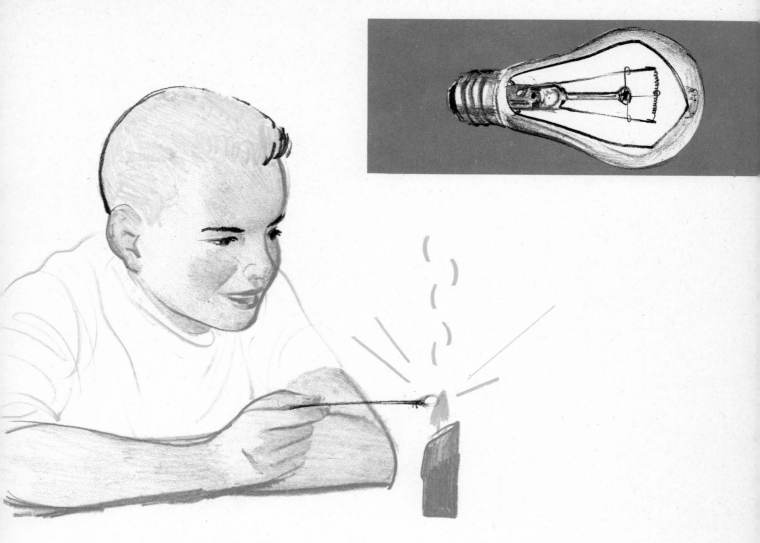

6. *What makes a light bulb light up? This experiment will help
you find out what makes an electric light bulb light up.*

Use a fine piece of iron picture wire about 6 inches
long. Make a loop about as big around as a lead pencil
at one end. Now put the loop in a flame. Notice what
happens. The loop becomes bright red. It gives off light.
Then it burns up.

The wire in an electric light bulb gets red hot because electricity is going through it. It does not burn up
because there is no oxygen in the bulb, and fire needs
oxygen in order to burn. There is either a vacuum in the
bulb or a gas that will not support fire.

The electricity you have been experimenting with is current electricity. There is another kind of electricity called static electricity. Another name for it is frictional electricity.

52

You may make some static electricity by rubbing a balloon which has been blown up. Now see whether the balloon will cling to the wall. It will cling because it has been charged with static electricity.

You might put a piece of tissue paper on a black board and rub it. It will stick to the black board until its charge is gone. Static electricity works best on a cold day.

8. *You may both hear and see static electricity if you do this experiment. How can I hear and see electricity?*

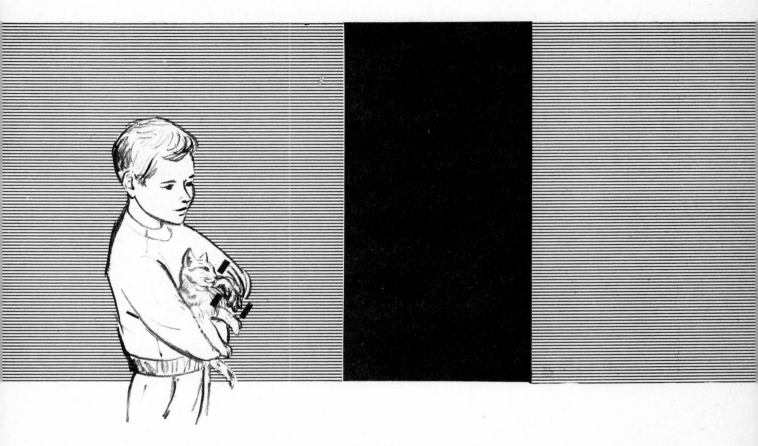

Take your favorite kitty with you into a cool dark room. (This will not hurt your kitty.) Gently rub your kitty's fur from his head down his back. Do this over and over always in the same direction. You are almost sure to see sparks of electricity. You will hear the electricity crackle, too.

You may both see and hear electricity when you shuffle your feet over a rug in the winter time and touch some object.

53

9. What do electric charges do to each other?

Put a silk thread through the end of a grain of puffed rice.

Tie the other end of the thread to a support so that the puffed rice will be hanging down 8 or more inches. Put a second one up in the same way so that the puffed rice grains are about even with each other.

Now rub a hard rubber rod or comb with flannel or fur. Hold the rod near to the puffed rice and notice what happens. The puffed rice will first jump to the rod. Then they push away from the rod and from each other. This happens because the puffed rice are first attracted to the rod. They get the charge of electricity which the rod has and then they are repelled. They push away from each other because they have the same charge of static electricity.

Charges of electricity which are alike repel each other. Charges which are not alike attract each other. The charges are called negative and positive. These charges were negative.

10. How can a positive charge of electricity be made?

Find four books each about an inch thick. Place two books in one pile on a table and the other two about a foot away in another pile. Place a glass window pane from one pile of books to another. Cut some tissue paper dolls about one-inch tall. Put the dolls under the glass. Rub the glass vigorously with a silk cloth. After a while the dolls will come up and touch the glass. Then they get the same charge as the glass (positive) and are repelled. They may start dancing up and down.

Each time they come up and touch the glass they get charged and each time they go down they lose their charge and are pulled back up again.

11. You have read that the positive electric charges attract the negative charge. This experiment will help you see it happen. What do a positive and negative charge do to each other?

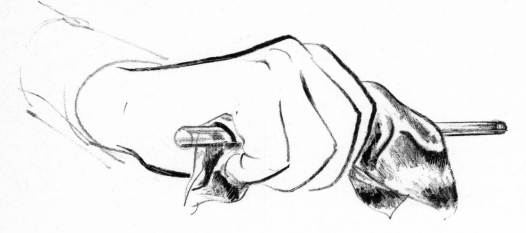

Rub a glass stirring rod hard with silk. With a silk thread suspend it in the air by tying it to a support. Now rub a hard rubber rod with fur. Hold the rubber rod close to the glass rod without touching it. Notice what happens.

The rubber rod has a negative charge and the glass rod a positive charge. They attract each other.

Now you know that:

Currents of electricity can be turned off and on with a switch.

A complete circuit is necessary to make a bell ring.

A short circuit may make a bell ring all the time.

Many metals are good conductors of electricity.

A fuse helps protect homes from fire.

A light bulb lights because the filament becomes very hot and gives off light.

Static electricity can be produced by rubbing.

Like electric charges repel each other.

Unlike electric charges attract each other.

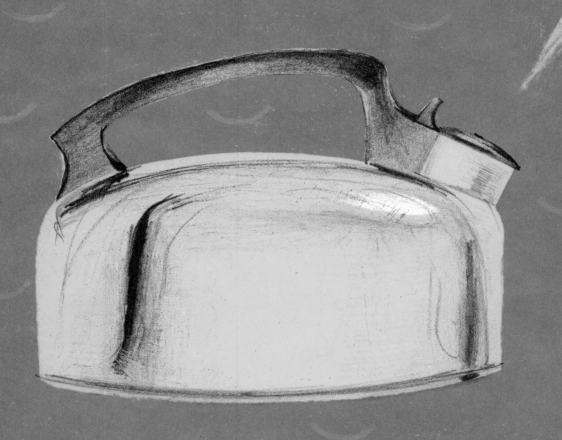

58

WATER

1. What happens to water left standing in a dish?

Find three dishes all alike. Put a teaspoonful of water in one dish, two teaspoonfuls of water in another dish, and three in the other. Place them side by side and let stand. Examine them every two or three hours. Notice what happens. The dish with one teaspoonful of water became empty first, then the one with two and then the one with three.

The water disappeared a little at a time into the air. We call this evaporation.

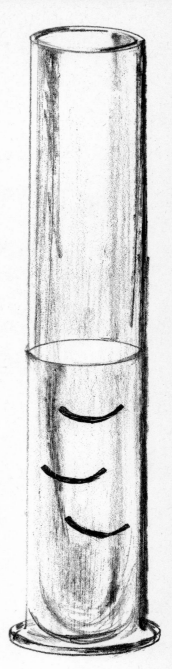

2. *From which of these dishes will water evaporate first?*

Find a saucer, a water glass and a footed test tube or narrow-necked bottle. Put 2 tablespoonfuls of water in each of them. Place them side by side and let stand. From which one did the water evaporate first? Which one was second? Try to think of a reason why this happened as it did. You are right if you say the water evaporated from the saucer first because the air touched more of it.

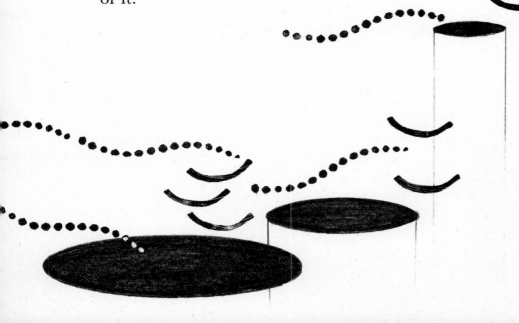

3. Does wind help water to evaporate?

Draw two squares on a blackboard. Be sure they are the the same size. Make each of them wet, by rubbing them with a wet cloth. Now fan one of them.

Which dries first? The one which was fanned is sure to dry first. The wind carries the particles of water away faster than the air which is not moving so fast does. The little particles of water are called molecules.

62

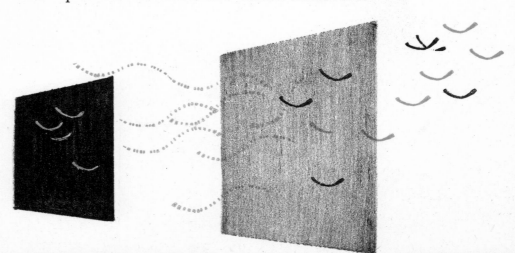

4. Does heat help water evaporate?

Use two towels that are exactly the same size and kind of material. Fold the two together and put them in water. This way they will each get exactly the same amount of water. Now hang one of the towels in a warm place and one of them in a cold place. Be sure there is no wind in either place. Notice which dries first.

The one in the warm place will probably dry first because the little molecules of water will go into warm air faster than into cold air. This is because the molecules of warm air are moving faster than molecules of cold air.

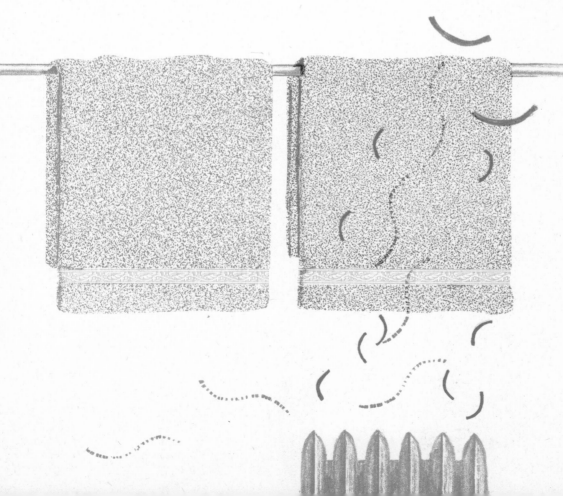

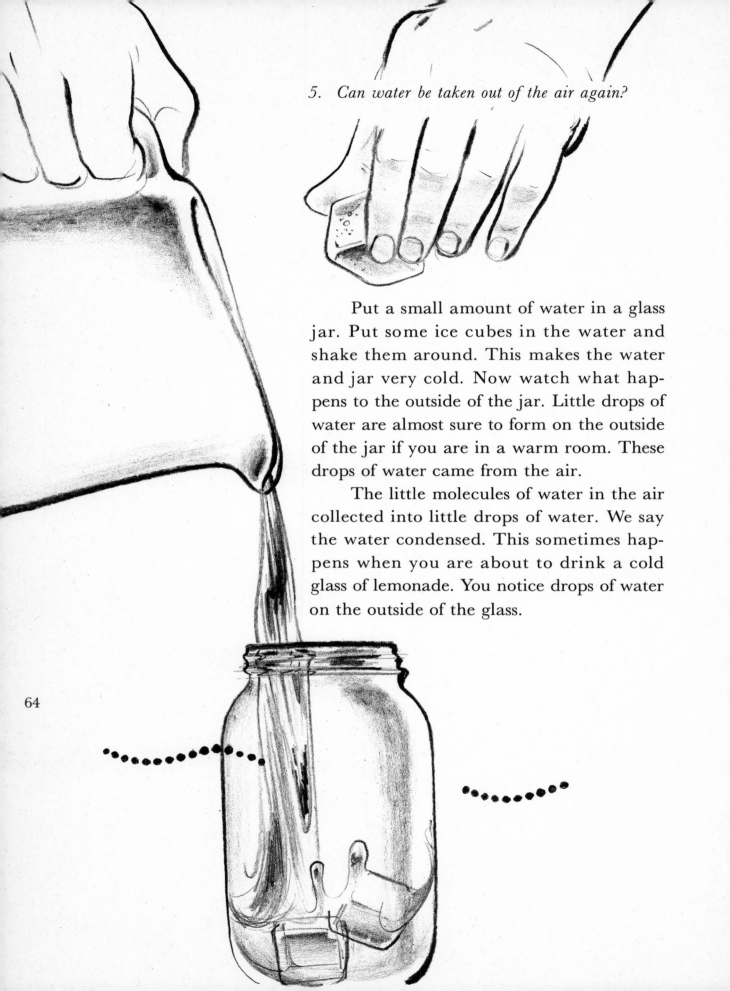

5. Can water be taken out of the air again?

Put a small amount of water in a glass jar. Put some ice cubes in the water and shake them around. This makes the water and jar very cold. Now watch what happens to the outside of the jar. Little drops of water are almost sure to form on the outside of the jar if you are in a warm room. These drops of water came from the air.

The little molecules of water in the air collected into little drops of water. We say the water condensed. This sometimes happens when you are about to drink a cold glass of lemonade. You notice drops of water on the outside of the glass.

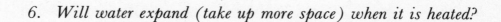

6. Will water expand (take up more space) when it is heated?

Use a flask, a one-hole rubber stopper with a glass tube through it. Fill the flask with water, colored with a little food coloring. The coloring makes it possible for you to see it more easily.

Heat the flask of water gently or slowly. Notice what happens. The water starts going up in the glass tube. This is because the molecules of water move faster and farther apart as they are heated. Then the water takes up more room and we say it "expands."

7. *You may wonder since doing experiment number 6 which is heavier, warm or cold water.*

Find two pint milk bottles of exactly the same size. Fill one of them with hot water and the other with cold water. Use food coloring to color the hot water.

Place a paper over the mouth of the milk bottle with cold water in it. Now hold the paper firm and turn the milk bottle upside down over the other one.

Pull the paper away from between the two bottles. Notice what happens. The warm water is lighter and gets pushed up by the heavier cold water. This experiment may cause you to wonder about ice and whether it sinks or floats.

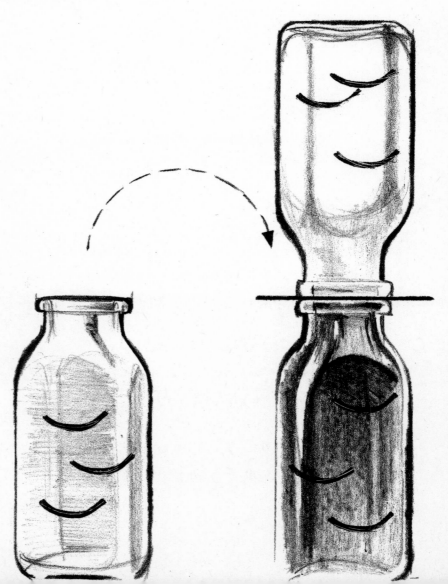

8. *Will ice float?*

Place about six ice cubes in a pan of water and watch them. Notice whether they sink or float. If the ice cubes float then how much of the cube is above water and about how much is below water? This shows you why ice-bergs are so dangerous. They float so that they are both above and below water and are not always easy to see. Ice floats because it is lighter than water.

Cold water contracts and gets heavier as it gets colder until it is near freezing—then there is a point at which it expands until it freezes. The temperature at which it starts to expand is about 4° C. This is not true of most things which become solids.

9. What does water do to sugar, salt and sand?

Put a tablespoonful of sugar in a cup of water and stir. What happens? Do the same with salt. What happens? Do the same with sand. What happens? The sugar and salt both dissolved in the water very quickly, but the sand did not.

10. *Will the sugar dissolve faster in hot water than in cold water?*

Use two glasses the same size. Put cold water in one of them and the same amount of hot water in the other. Put one tablespoonful of sugar in the hot water and see how long it takes for the sugar to dissolve.

Now put the same amount of sugar in the cold water and see how long it takes for it to dissolve. The sugar dissolved faster in the hot water. The molecules of water are moving about faster in the hot water.

11. *What happens to the sugar when water evaporates?*

Fill a cup one-half full of hot water. Stir into the water three tablespoons of sugar. Now place two tablespoons of the sugar solution in a saucer and let stand. After the water has evaporated what is left in the saucer? You will find sugar in the saucer. The water evaporated but the sugar did not.

70

Now you know that:

Water evaporates.

The greater the water surface the quicker the water will
evaporate.

Wind speeds up evaporation.

Heat speeds up evaporation.

Water vapor will condense where it is cooled.

Water will expand when it is heated.

Warm water is lighter than cold water.

Ice will float.

Water dissolves some things quickly.

Hot water dissolves things faster than cold water.

When water evaporates from sugar water, sugar stays
in the container.

72

HEAT

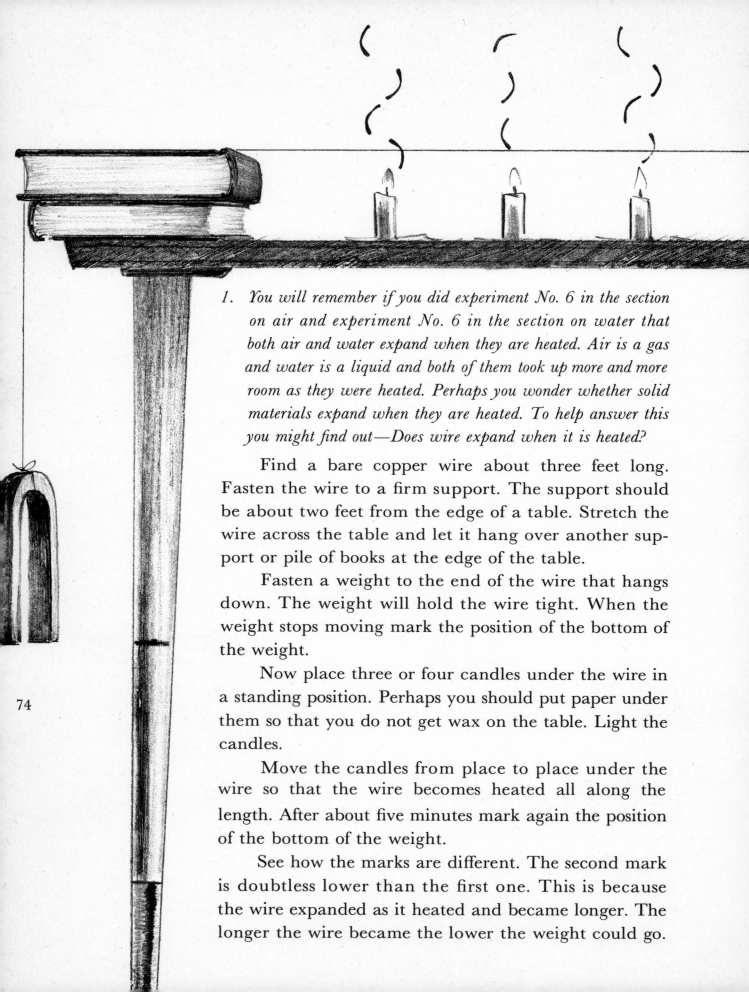

1. *You will remember if you did experiment No. 6 in the section on air and experiment No. 6 in the section on water that both air and water expand when they are heated. Air is a gas and water is a liquid and both of them took up more and more room as they were heated. Perhaps you wonder whether solid materials expand when they are heated. To help answer this you might find out—Does wire expand when it is heated?*

Find a bare copper wire about three feet long. Fasten the wire to a firm support. The support should be about two feet from the edge of a table. Stretch the wire across the table and let it hang over another support or pile of books at the edge of the table.

Fasten a weight to the end of the wire that hangs down. The weight will hold the wire tight. When the weight stops moving mark the position of the bottom of the weight.

Now place three or four candles under the wire in a standing position. Perhaps you should put paper under them so that you do not get wax on the table. Light the candles.

Move the candles from place to place under the wire so that the wire becomes heated all along the length. After about five minutes mark again the position of the bottom of the weight.

See how the marks are different. The second mark is doubtless lower than the first one. This is because the wire expanded as it heated and became longer. The longer the wire became the lower the weight could go.

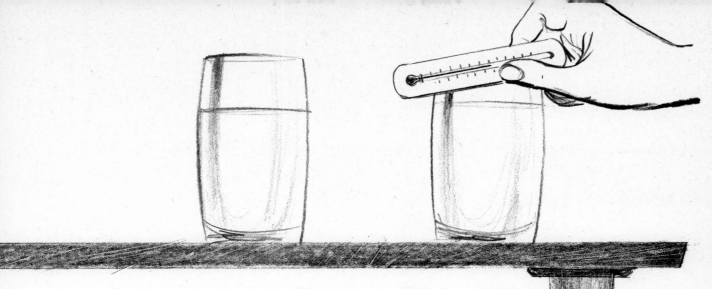

2. Our bodies are sensitive to heat and cold. We know whether we are warm or cold. We might then ask ourselves—Why are thermometers so often used to determine the temperature of a place or thing?

Get a glass of water from the faucet. Feel of it and try to determine for yourself the temperature. Write down your estimate.

Now use a thermometer and find out the actual temperature. Do this again and see whether you were right.

Try this same experiment using hot water. Do you think that you were a good thermometer? You probably think that your estimates cannot be depended upon completely.

Neither can we be depended upon to judge temperatures of rooms. If we come in from the cold outside we probably think the room is warm. If we come into the same room from the hot outside we probably think that the room is cool.

Exact temperatures can only be found by the use of a thermometer.

3. How can I make a thermometer?

Use a Florence flask, a one-hole rubber stopper, and a piece of glass tubing. Dampen the rubber stopper and the glass tubing. Put the end of the tubing into the hole of the stopper. Now put the stopper into the flask so that it is air tight, except for the air which goes through the tube.

Turn the flask upside down and put the end of the tube in some water. Fix a support for the flask so that it will be held in position.

You may wish to color the water so that you can see what happens more easily. Add a bit of food coloring to color it.

Hold your hands on the ball of the flask until the air in it has expanded enough that a few (8-10) bubbles of air have escaped. Now you have an air thermometer. When the air gets colder the water in the tube goes up. This is because the air in the bulb contracted and took up less room. When the air gets warmer and expands, the air in the tube goes down. This can be called an upside-down thermometer because it works in the opposite direction from the regular thermometers—the bulb is up instead of down. A man by the name of Galileo invented this air thermometer.

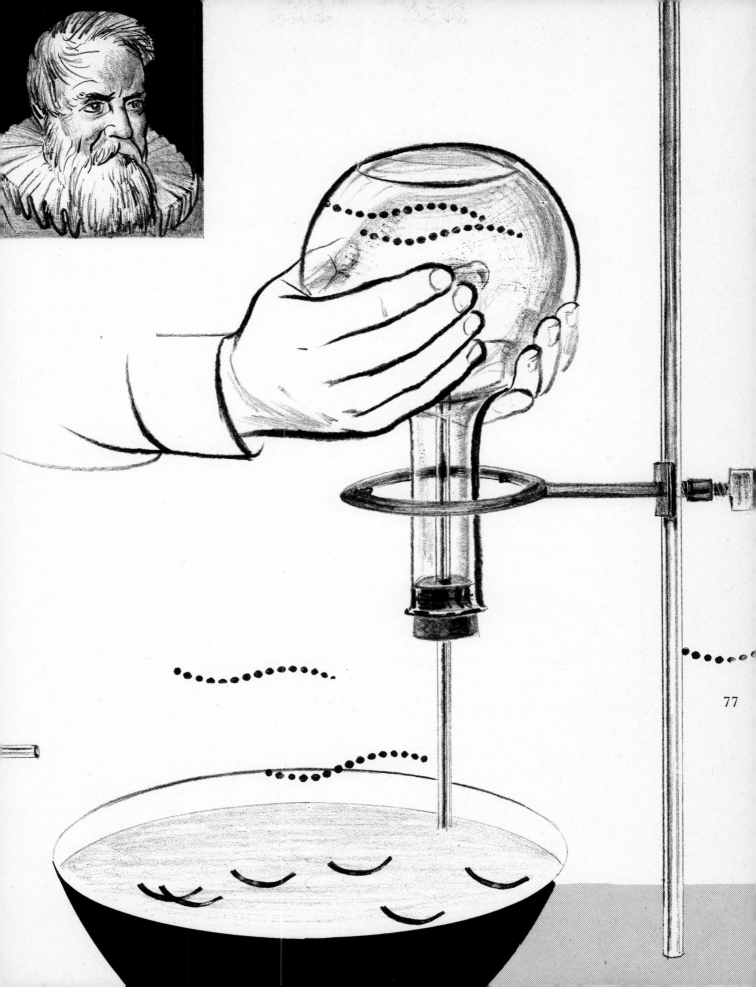

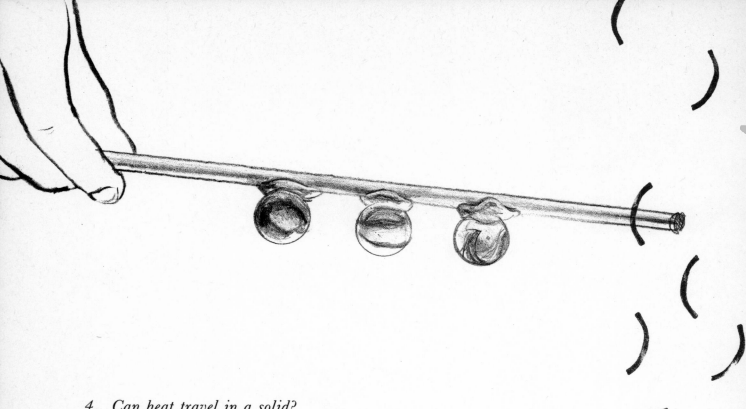

4. Can heat travel in a solid?

Use a metal curtain rod one foot or more long. Find a candle and three marbles. Light the candle and drip a little wax on the rod about two inches from the end of the rod. Before the wax hardens hold one of the marbles in it. The wax will harden and fasten the marble to the rod.

In the same way fasten another marble on the rod one inch from the first marble. It will then be about three inches from the end.

The third marble can be fastened one inch from the last—four inches from the end.

Hold the end of the rod nearest the marbles in a flame and see what happens to the marbles. Which fell off first, second, third? It is easy to see from this that heat can travel through solids.

It is easy to see, too, that the heat travels away from the source of heat.

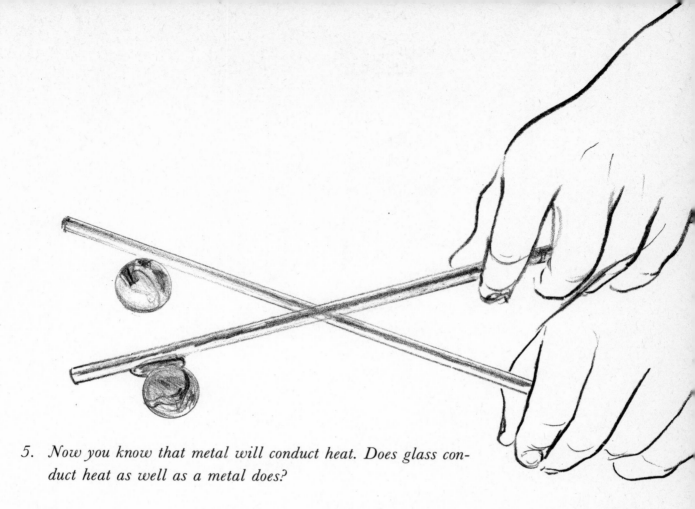

5. *Now you know that metal will conduct heat. Does glass conduct heat as well as a metal does?*

Find a glass stirring rod and a metal rod as nearly the same diameter as possible.

Fasten a marble with candle wax about one inch from the end of each one of them.

Now hold the end of the metal rod in the flame and see how long it takes for the marble to fall off.

Now hold the glass rod in the flame and see how long it takes the marble to fall off. You should try this experiment more than once to find out whether the same thing always happens each time.

Doubtless you decided that the metal rod was the better conductor of heat because the marble on the metal rod fell off first almost every time.

Metal is a better conductor of heat than glass is. This is why we put hot food in metal pans if we wish it to cool quickly.

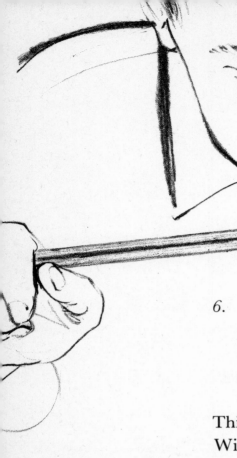

6. *Now you may wonder whether all metals are equally good conductors. You might find a copper rod, a brass rod, and an aluminum one and then ask this question—Which is the best conductor of heat—copper, brass or aluminum?*

This experiment can be done just as number 5 was done. With candle wax fasten a marble about one inch from the end of each rod. Hold the rods one at a time in a flame and time it to see how long it takes for the marble to fall off of each one. You will be wise to repeat this experiment several times. Although you intend to get the same amount of wax on each one it is not always possible.

Of course the amount of wax has a great deal to do with the length of time which it will take for the marble to fall off. You will come to the conclusion that copper is a better conductor than either of the others because probably the marble fell off first almost every time.

80

You will probably decide that aluminum is a better conductor than brass because in most of the experiments the marble on the aluminum rod fell off second.

7. *Can you hold a test tube with water in it while the water is boiling? You are almost sure to say no to this question. Try this experiment.*

Fill a test tube (Be sure the test tube is Pyrex) about three-fourths full of water. Hold the bottom of the tube in your thumb and front finger. Hold the tube so that the flame hits the tube where the top of the water is. See whether you could hold the tube until the water boiled.

Do you understand why you were able to do it? Remember that glass is a poor conductor of heat and that hot water is lighter than cold water and you will be able to explain why you were able to do it.

8. Why do we wear wool in the winter time or when it is cold?

Find two pint milk bottles which are just alike. Get a pitcher of hot water and take the temperature of the water. Record the temperature so that you will not forget it.

Pour some of the hot water into one of the milk bottles and some of it into the other milk bottle so that both of them are full to the top. Put a cork in each of them. Wrap one of them with a woolen cloth and then set them side by side in a cool place.

After about one-half hour take the temperature of the water in each milk bottle. How did they compare? The one with the wool around it was warmer because wool is a poor conductor of heat. It did not let so much of the heat in the bottle escape.

We wear woolen clothing so that the heat from our bodies will not escape so easily. Wool is a poor conductor because it has many little air spaces in it.

82

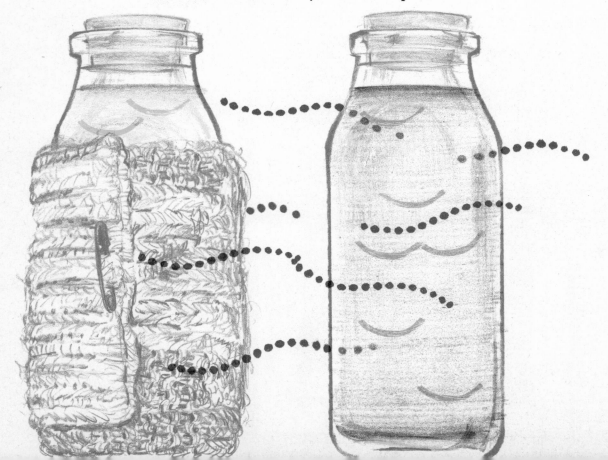

9.   Why do we wear light colored clothing in the summer time?

Use two test tubes the same size. Fill a glass with cold water. Take the temperature of the water. Fill the two test tubes with water from the glass. Wrap one of the test tubes with white paper and the other black paper. Place the test tubes side by side in the sunshine.

After about thirty minutes take the temperature of the water in each of the test tubes. The water in the test tube wrapped in black will have absorbed some of the heat from the sun and will be warmer than the other. The white paper will reflect more of the heat than the black paper does.

We are cooler in the summer time if we wear light-colored clothing. The light-colored clothing will reflect the heat from the sun better than the dark color will.

10. *Why do we feel cool when we come from swimming in the summer time?*

Let a bottle of water and a bottle of alcohol stand side by side over night. Put a drop of water on a saucer and a drop of alcohol in another place on the same saucer and notice which disappears first. The alcohol will disappear first because it evaporates faster. Now put a couple of drops of water on the back of your hand and a couple of drops of alcohol on the back of your other hand.

How does each of them feel? The alcohol will doubtless feel cooler. It feels cooler because it evaporates faster. As a liquid evaporates, heat is taken from your hand. You probably remember that wind speeds up evaporation.

When you come out of the pool the air and maybe wind hits your body and speeds up the evaporation and because it is evaporating fast you feel cool.

84

Now you know that:

Wire expands when it is heated.

We need thermometers to measure temperature accurately.

Heat travels through solids.

Glass is a poor conductor of heat.

Some metals are better conductors than others.

Wool is a poor conductor of heat.

Dark colors absorb heat and light colors reflect it.

Evaporation has a cooling effect.

SOUND

1. *What causes sound?*

Place one end of a ruler on the edge of the table so that the other end extends beyond the table. Notice that there is no sound.

Now hit the free end of the ruler and notice what you hear and see.

Stretch the rubber band over an empty box. Notice there is no sound. Now pluck the rubber band. Watch and listen for what happens.

Hold the piece of paper up to your lips and blow on the edge of it. What do you hear and see?

Hold the tuning fork motionless. Feel it and listen to it. Now hit one tine of the fork lightly on something solid. Watch and listen to the fork. Hit the fork again and feel of it. What do you notice?

It was easy to see that something moved back and forth when the sounds were made. This shows that sounds are caused by vibrations. When something moves back and forth we say it vibrates. The sounds which are made when something vibrates travels to our ears through the air.

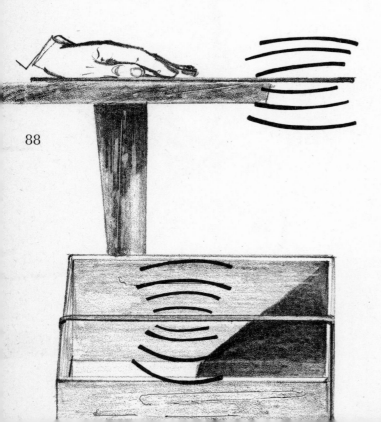

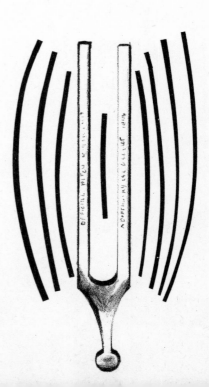

2. *Now you have learned that sound is caused by vibrations. You have learned, too, that vibrations travel through air. You are probably wondering whether sound vibrations travel through other kinds of materials. You might do an experiment and answer this question:*

Will sound vibrations travel through wood?

Sit at a table which is made of wood. Tap the table lightly with a pencil and listen carefully to the sound. As you continue to tap the table lower your head to the table and listen with one ear on the table top.

Try this experiment several times. You will decide that the sound is louder when you hear it through the wood of the table top. Wood not only carries sound but carries it better than air does.

Your next question will probably be—Will metal carry sound better than wood? You may plan an experiment for yourself and answer that question. You will find out that metal does carry sound better than wood.

*3. Now we know that sounds are caused by vibra-
tions. Here is another question which you are
almost sure to ask yourself.*

*Do our ears help catch sound waves? Try
this experiment.*

Listen to a person talking or to a piece
of music for one minute. Notice how loud
the sound is. Now place one hand behind
each ear and cup the hands forward. Listen
again. Now notice how loud the sound is.

Place a finger on each ear and hold the
ear back against the head. Listen again.
Now notice how loud the sound is. The
sound was louder when you held your hands
behind your ears than it was when you first
listened. When you held your ears back
against your head the sound was not so loud
as when you first listened. You can see that
the ears do help catch the sound waves.

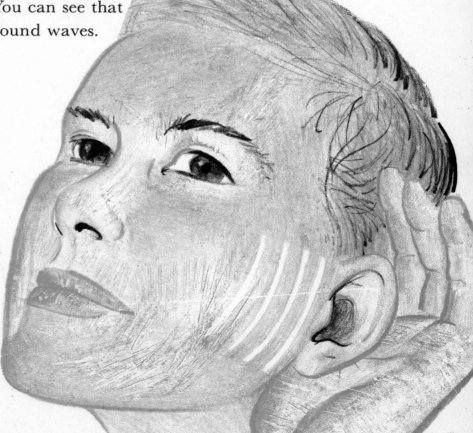

4. What makes some sounds louder than others?

Try hitting a drum very lightly and notice the sound.

Hit it a bit harder and notice the sound.

Hit it very hard and notice the sound.

You have decided that the harder it is hit the louder the sound. When the drum is hit hard the skin goes back and forth farther than when it is not hit so hard.

The loudness of a sound depends upon how big the vibrations are. Sounds are louder or not so loud depending upon what the vibration travels through, too.

There are other things which affect the loudness of sounds. How good a person's ears are and how far they are from the sound also affects the loudness.

5. *What causes sounds to be different pitch?*

Place the rubber bands around the smaller of the two boxes. Pluck one of them and notice the sounds Now pluck the other of them and notice the sound. The thicker rubber band makes a lower sound than the other.

Now put the two rubber bands around the bigger box. Pluck them. The sounds are higher than they were on the smaller box. The rubber bands had to be stretched tighter to get them over the larger box. The thickness of the rubber bands and the tightness of them have to do with the pitch. The pitch is higher if it is stretched tighter and if it is a finer rubber band.

You might try planning an experiment to find out whether the length of the string has anything to do with the pitch. You will find out that length affects the pitch. The pitch is higher when the rubber band is shorter than when it is longer.

92

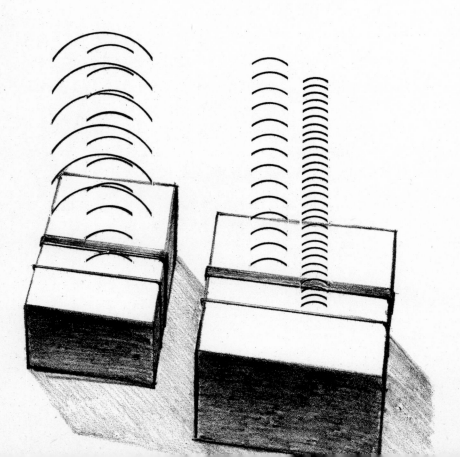

Now you know that:

Sounds are caused by vibrations.

Sound travels better through wood than it does through
air.

Ears help catch sound waves.

Some sounds are louder than others because the waves
go back and forth farther than others.

Some sounds are higher than others because the waves
are faster than others.

LIGHT

1. How does light get from one place to another?

Find a piece of glass about 6″ square. Cut a piece of black paper the same size. Cut a piece of wax paper that size.

Now light a lamp and hold the glass between you and the lamp. Now hold the wax paper up between you and the lamp. Try the black paper in the same way. You doubtless discovered light went through the glass and you could see through it. Light went through the wax paper but you could not see through it. Light did not go through the black paper and you, of course, could not see through it.

The glass is said to be transparent. The wax paper is said to be translucent and the black paper opaque.

Now cut a circle in the black paper and then hold it to the lamp and notice the shadow it makes. The shadow is round like the circle and square like the paper. Light travels in a straight line and it cannot go through the black paper, so you see the lighted circle and the black shadow.

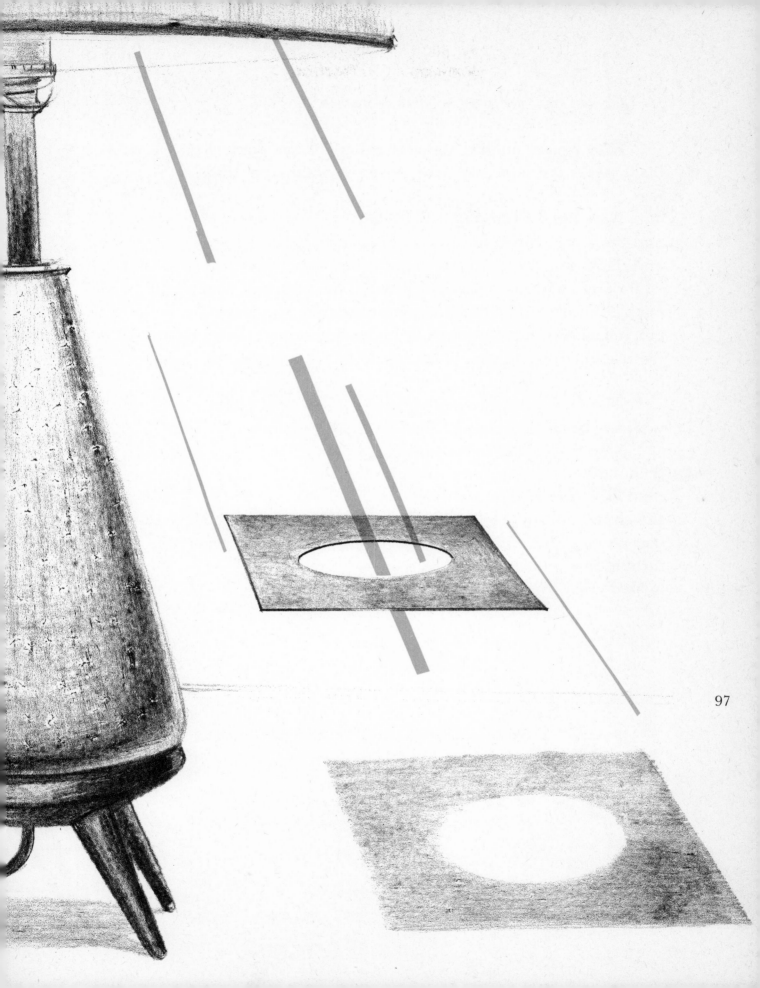

2. *Here is another experiment which will help you understand how light gets from one place to another.*

Stand in a window and use a mirror. Hold the mirror in such a way that the bright sunlight hits it. Move it slowly about. You will find a reflection of the sunlight on the wall.

As you move the mirror slowly, the sunlight on the wall moves. The rays of light come from the sun—hit the mirror—and are bounced or reflected to the place on the wall. The light travels in a straight line to the mirror and in a straight line to the wall where you see it.

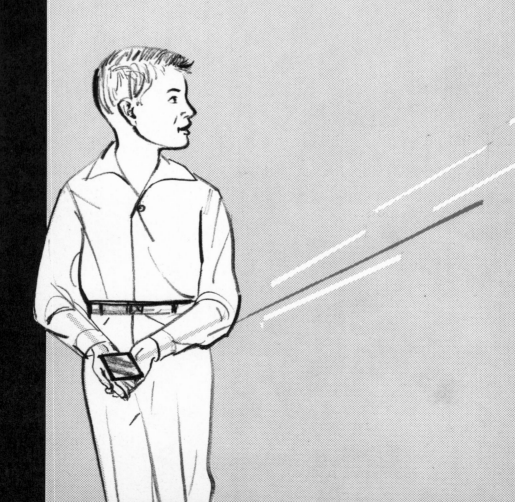

3. *What kinds of things reflect the most light?*

Place a piece of white paper and a piece of black paper side by side on a table. Each piece should be at least six inches square. Darken the room. With a flashlight, point a light on the black paper and notice the amount of light in the room. Point the light on the white paper and notice again the amount of light in the room. The white paper reflects more light. Try the experiment with papers of other colors. Try it with rough surfaces and polished surfaces. You will find that smooth, light-colored things reflect more light than rough, dark ones. Some kinds of things reflect light better than others.

99

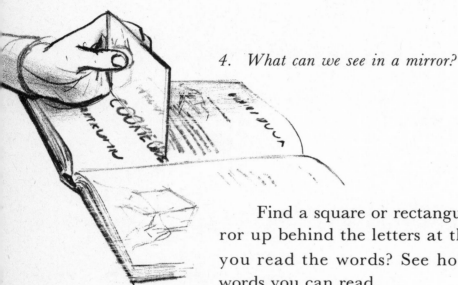

4. What can we see in a mirror?

Find a square or rectangular mirror. Stand the mirror up behind the letters at the top of this page. Could you read the words? See how many of the following words you can read.

The mirror bends the light rays which come to it so that the letter appears upside down in the mirror. The upside down half with the half on the paper completes the image. In some cases the image was a word. COOKIE, OBOE, and OHIO could be read. Can you think of other words which can be read?

100

COOKIE OBOE

MIRROR OHIO

5. Can we get a reflection of a reflection?

Stick a pin into a pad of paper. Take a rectangular mirror in each of your hands and stand them up so that they are side by side with the pin in front of the place where they touch each other.

Now move the outer edges of the mirrors slowly forward. You will see that you have more than one pin. You may have as many as eight reflections of the pin. In fact, you have reflections of reflections.

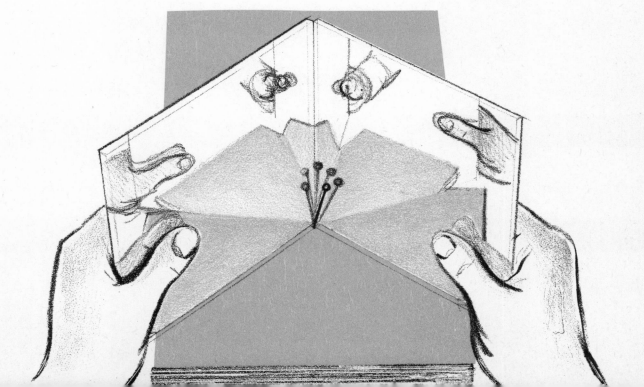

6. *What is refraction? This experiment will help you under-stand what refraction is.*

Fill a glass two thirds full of water. Stand a spoon in the glass of water. The handle of the spoon will appear broken where the surface of the water touches it. The top part of the spoon looks to be where it really is because the rays of light reflected from it go only through the air and glass.

The lower part of the spoon appears to be moved over—not where it really is—because the rays reflected from it go through both the water and air. The rays are bent. This we call refraction. Other things will refract light. Glass is one of them. The lenses in glasses are cut so they will refract or bend light rays in just the right way to help the eyes to see. There are many uses of light refraction.

7. How can we make a rainbow?

Hold a prism in the path of a ray of sunlight and turn the prism slowly until you see a rainbow on the wall or ceiling.

If you succeed in putting the rainbow on a table, lay a piece of white paper where the rainbow lies. You will notice it shows up more clearly on the white. The sunlight is made up of the rainbow colors—violet, indigo, blue, green, yellow, orange and red. The prism is glass cut into a particular shape. Because of this shape it separates the white sunlight into the rainbow colors.

You may be able to get a rainbow in another way.

Set a glass dish of water in the sunlight. You may see a rainbow on the wall. The water breaks the sunlight up into the colors of which it is made. This is why we have rainbows. The sunshine on drops of water in the sky may cause a rainbow which we can see.

104

Now you know that:

Light travels through some materials and not through
others.

Light can be reflected.

Light travels in a straight line.

Smooth, light-colored things reflect the most light.

A mirror bends the light rays that come to it.

We can get a reflection of a reflection.

Light rays are bent as they go through some materials.

Light rays can be broken into the colors of the rainbow.

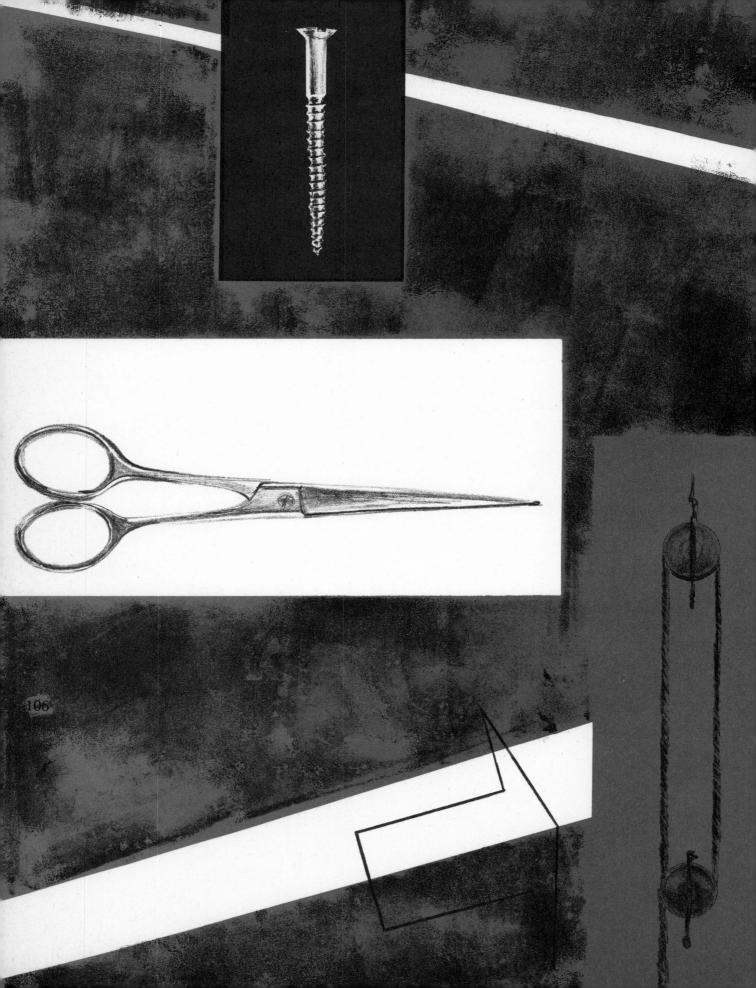

MACHINES

1. How can a heavy box of toys be moved from one side of a room to the other?

Find two broom sticks. Put one of them under the front end of the box and the other nearer the back end of it. Now the box will roll forward easily. The box will roll off of the broomstick nearer the back. This broom stick may be put under the front of the box and the box rolled forward again.

Each time the box rolls off of one of the broom sticks put it under the front and continue moving the box. The broom sticks serve as wheels. They made the work a great deal easier.

2. *It is easy to tell that the work is made easier by using the broom sticks in experiment No. 1. How can we measure the amount of work which wheels do?*

Use a small toy cart and a spring balance scales. You may need to borrow the spring balance scales from a science laboratory.

Tie a string to the front of the toy cart. Hook the spring balance scales to the other end of the string. Now turn the cart upside down on the floor and pull it along paying attention to the reading on the spring balance scales. The reading will tell you how much work you are doing.

Turn the cart over on its wheels and pull it along again. Notice the reading on the spring balance scales. It will be a great deal less because the wheels are doing much of the work for you.

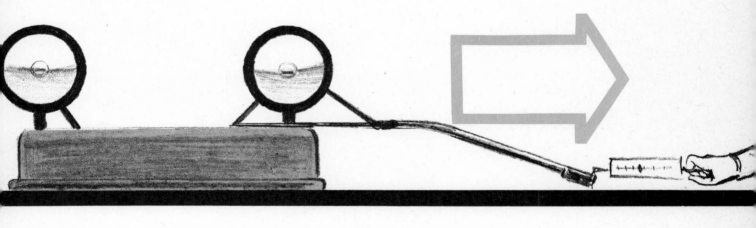

3. *Wheels are called simple machines because they do work for us. There are other kinds of simple machines. Suppose your family was moving. How could you get your heavy bicycle up into the truck? You could use an inclined plane. How does an inclined plane help do work?*

For this experiment you will need the spring balance and the little toy cart which you used in experiment No. 2. You will also need a board at least six inches wide and three feet long.

Lay the board on the floor. Set the cart at one end of it. Fasten the spring balance on the end of the string which is on the cart and pull the cart along the board. Notice how much force it takes to pull the cart. The amount of force will be the reading on the spring balance. This is the amount of work which you are doing. Now hold the spring balance so that the cart is dangling at the other end of the string from it. Notice the reading on the spring balance.

This is the weight of the cart and the measure of the work which you are doing.

Arrange the board so that one end of it is on the floor and the other end is on a pile of books about one foot high. Now pull the cart up the board and notice the reading on the spring balance. You will notice that you are working harder than when the board was on the floor but not so hard as when you lifted it straight up in the air.

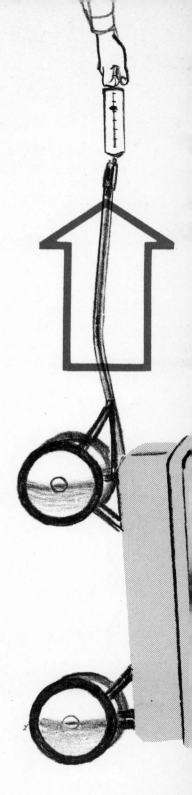

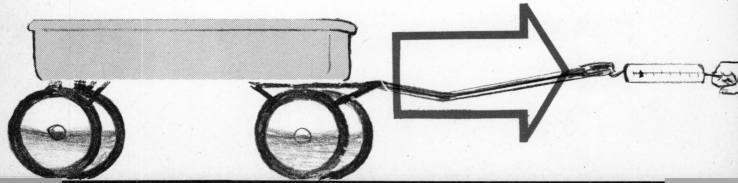

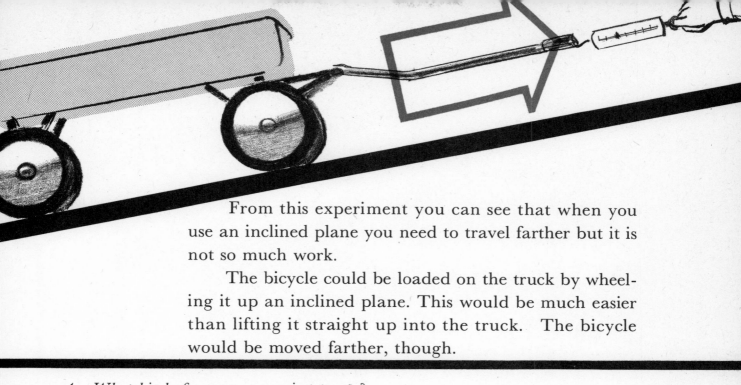

From this experiment you can see that when you use an inclined plane you need to travel farther but it is not so much work.

The bicycle could be loaded on the truck by wheeling it up an inclined plane. This would be much easier than lifting it straight up into the truck. The bicycle would be moved farther, though.

4. What kind of screws are easiest to use?

Find two screws which are the same length and the same size around. The one difference in these two screws should be that one of them has many more threads than the other. The picture will help you understand what threads are.

Find a board at least three inches square and about as thick as the screws are long. With a hammer give each of the screws the same kind of a start into the wood. Use a screw driver and screw one of them down until it is about ¼ of its length in the wood. As you do it notice how hard it is to do. Notice, too, how many turns you make to put the screw in that far. Now screw the other one down and notice how this one compares to the other one. Screw each of them down until they are half in the wood.

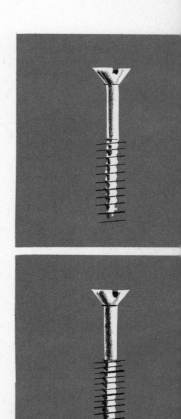

Was it the same one which was hardest to get in the wood? Was it the same one which took more turns to get it into the wood? Which one was the hardest, which one took the more turns? The one with more threads was doubtless easier but you had to turn it more times. Here, as in experiment No. 3, you must move farther but the work is easier.

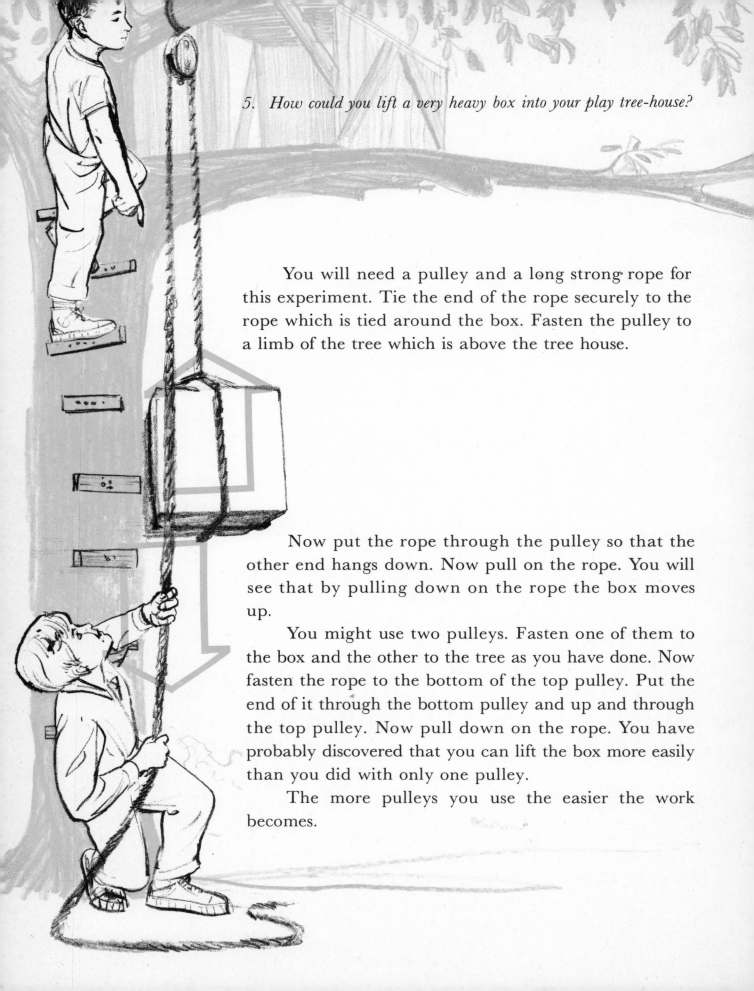

5. *How could you lift a very heavy box into your play tree-house?*

You will need a pulley and a long strong rope for this experiment. Tie the end of the rope securely to the rope which is tied around the box. Fasten the pulley to a limb of the tree which is above the tree house.

Now put the rope through the pulley so that the other end hangs down. Now pull on the rope. You will see that by pulling down on the rope the box moves up.

You might use two pulleys. Fasten one of them to the box and the other to the tree as you have done. Now fasten the rope to the bottom of the top pulley. Put the end of it through the bottom pulley and up and through the top pulley. Now pull down on the rope. You have probably discovered that you can lift the box more easily than you did with only one pulley.

The more pulleys you use the easier the work becomes.

Now you know that:

Wheels make work easier.

Inclined planes make work easier.

Screws make work easier.

Pulleys make work easier.

Wheels, inclined planes, screws, and pulleys are all simple machines.

CHEMISTRY

1. What happens when things rust?

Use a fairly large test tube from a chemistry set for this experiment. Fill the test tube with water and then empty the water. While the test tube is wet on the inside put a few iron filings in the tube and shake them around. Many of them will stick to the side of the tube. Empty the rest of them out. Now turn the test tube upside down and stand it in a dish which has about one-half inch of water in it.

Look at this test tube the next day. You will notice that water rises in the test tube. This must mean that some of the air has been used up. If you did experiment No. 10 in the section on air you probably remember that some of the air was used up as the candle burned. The part of the air which the fire used and the part which the rusting used was the same. It was the gas called oxygen. About one fifth of the air is oxygen. Rusting is, in a way, like very slow burning. In both cases oxygen is combining with something. In rusting, iron unites with the oxygen to form rust. Water came about one fifth of the way up in the tube and filled the place where the oxygen was. This experiment can be done with steel wool instead of iron filings.

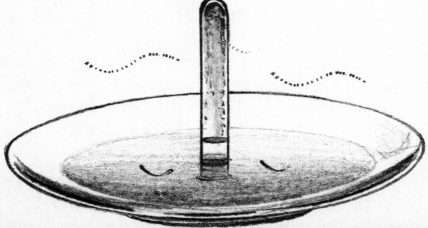

2. What happens when a candle burns?

Find a candle which has not been used before and place it in a candle holder. Light a match and bring it toward the candle wick from above. The wick starts burning after you have touched it with the lighted match.

Let the candle burn for a few minutes. Hold, in one hand, a candle snuffer or a teaspoon to put out the flame, and hold in the other hand a lighted match. Put out the flame and immediately bring the lighted match slowly toward the wick from above. Try this several times.

You will notice that the wick will catch fire before the match touches it. This is because the wick is surrounded with a gas that starts burning. When the wick is first lighted the heat from the burning wick melts the candle wax. The candle wax soon rises in the wick and is changed to gas. It is this gas which burns and causes the candle to give off light. When the candle was put out, the gas continued to be formed and when the lighted match was lowered near the wick the gas began to burn before the flame really touched the wick. When a candle burns it is really burning gas formed from the melted wax of the candle.

117

3. *How can we make Carbon Dioxide?*

Use three small beakers or glasses. In one of them put two tablespoonsful of baking soda. Fill another one-fourth full of vinegar and the third one one-fourth full of water. Light a match and hold it into each of the beakers one after the other. You will notice that the match continues to burn as long as there is enough of it to burn.

Now pour one-half of the water into the beaker of vinegar and the other half into the beaker of soda. Again light a match and hold it into the beaker of soda water and the beaker of vinegar water. Again the match continues to burn in each of them.

Pour the vinegar water into the soda water and notice what happens. Light a match and hold it into the beaker of vinegar soda water. This time the match goes out. You notice a lot of bubbles when the vinegar water was poured into the soda water. These bubbles were bubbles of carbon dioxide. The carbon dioxide held oxygen away from the flame and a flame cannot burn without oxygen. This is one way to make carbon dioxide.

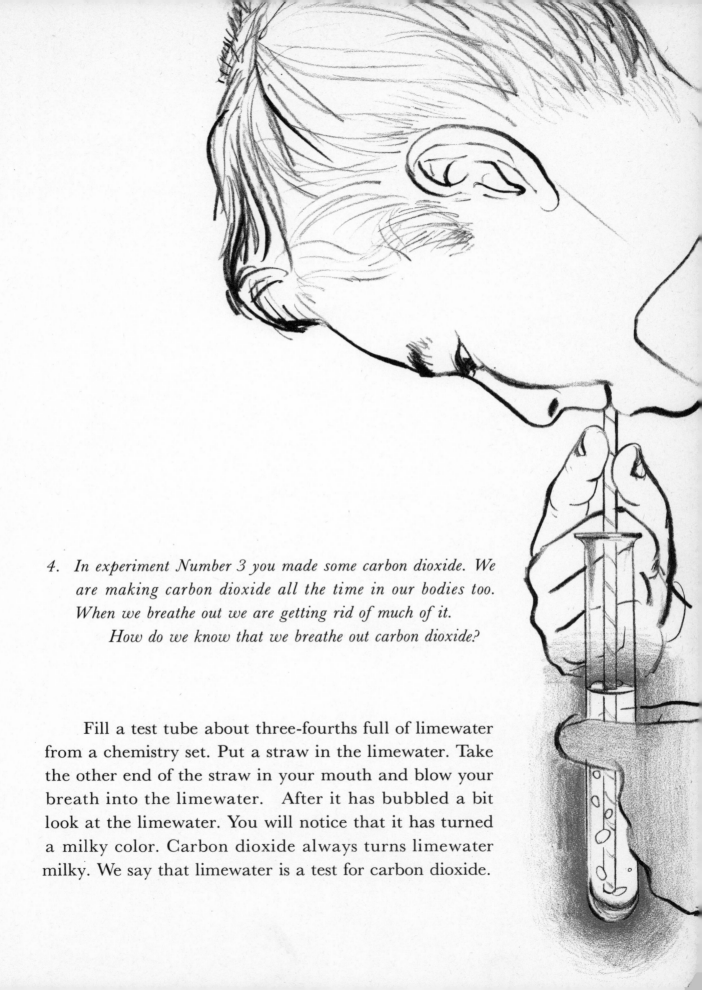

4. *In experiment Number 3 you made some carbon dioxide. We are making carbon dioxide all the time in our bodies too. When we breathe out we are getting rid of much of it.*

    How do we know that we breathe out carbon dioxide?

Fill a test tube about three-fourths full of limewater from a chemistry set. Put a straw in the limewater. Take the other end of the straw in your mouth and blow your breath into the limewater. After it has bubbled a bit look at the limewater. You will notice that it has turned a milky color. Carbon dioxide always turns limewater milky. We say that limewater is a test for carbon dioxide.

5. *Many of our foods have starch in them. How do we know if a food has starch in it?*

Dust a bit of cornstarch over a piece of glass. Dust a bit of baking soda over another piece of glass. Drop a drop of tincture of iodine on each of them. Compare them. The one which we know to be starch looks purple or almost black. The other one remains the color of the iodine. If starch is present we may expect the purple color. Try this test on scrapings from a potato, scrapings from an apple, a slice of white bread and a cracker. You will find that all of these foods, except the apple, have starch in them.

120

6. *Many of our foods have fats in them. How can we test for fats?*

Use a clean sheet of paper. Draw two small circles on the paper—one near each end. Rub some butter which we all know to be fat on one of the circles. In the circle at the end of the paper rub some lemon juice which we know not to be fat. Examine the paper after about ten minutes. Look at both sides of it. The place where the lemon juice was put is drying. It may not show on the back of the paper. The place where the butter was put will look greasy. The spot will spread and become larger. In this way test peanut butter, honey, and cream for fat. You will decide that the honey does not have fat in it. It made the paper sticky but not greasy. The other two made the paper greasy. This is called the spot test for fat.

121

7. *In experiment Number 5 we found that potatoes have a great deal of starch in them. Do potatoes have other substances in them?*

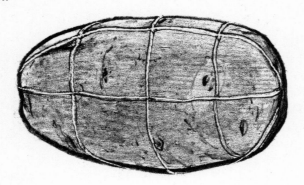

Use a scale which weighs very small amounts. Get a potato and wash it clean so that there will be no dirt to rub away. Now cut the potato into small pieces and write down the date and the total amount all these pieces of potato weighed. This will be about the same as the weight of the whole potato. On the next day weigh the potato again and write down the weight. You will notice that the potato weighed much less. This is because some of the water in the potato evaporated into the air. On each following day weigh the potato again until the weight of the potato does not change. When the weight does not change we will know that the potato has lost its water. From this experiment you are sure to decide that potatoes have much water in them.

122

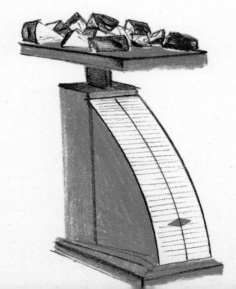

8. How do we test for acids?

In most chemistry sets there is litmus paper. Litmus paper is used to test for acids and for bases. Get a small amount of each of the following—vinegar, water, lemon juice, sweet milk, and liquid soap. Select 5 pieces of blue litmus paper. Put the end of each of these papers into each of the liquids and remove them again. Notice what happens. The vinegar and lemon juice caused them to turn pink. The other three remained the same. Blue litmus paper can be used to test for acids. It turns pink when acid is present. Select 5 pieces of pink litmus paper and test each of the liquids in the same way. Here you notice only one of them changed. The one with the liquid soap on it turned blue. Liquid soap is a base. Bases turn pink litmus paper blue. The other liquids, milk and water, changed the color of neither paper because they were neither acids nor bases.

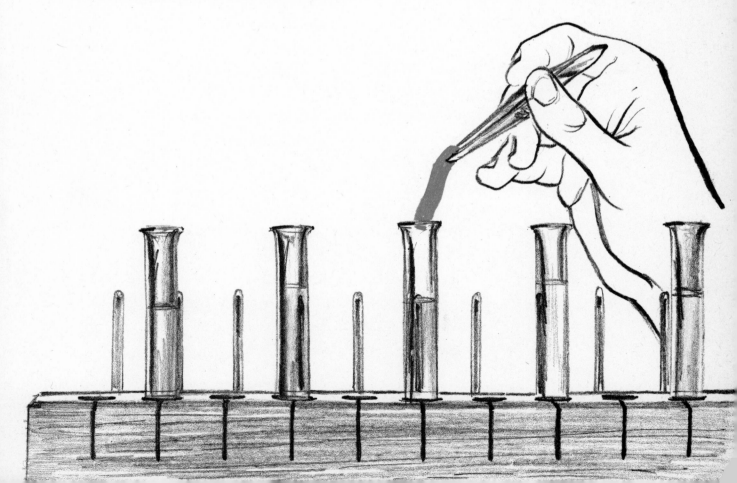

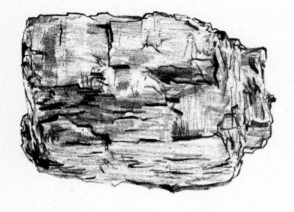

COAL

LIMESTONE

9. *How can we test for lime in rocks?*

Find a piece of limestone, a piece of granite, and a piece of coal. We know that limestone has lime and that the other two do not. Put a drop of hydrochloric acid on each of these rocks. You will notice that there are bubbles on the limestone but not on the other two rocks. This is the test—when there is lime present there will be bubbles of carbon dioxide formed when the acid test is used. Try the test on three other rocks—marble, coral rock and slate. You will decide that the marble and coral rock both have lime in them. This is not surprising since marble is formed from limestone and limestone is formed from shells and other remains of sea animals.

124

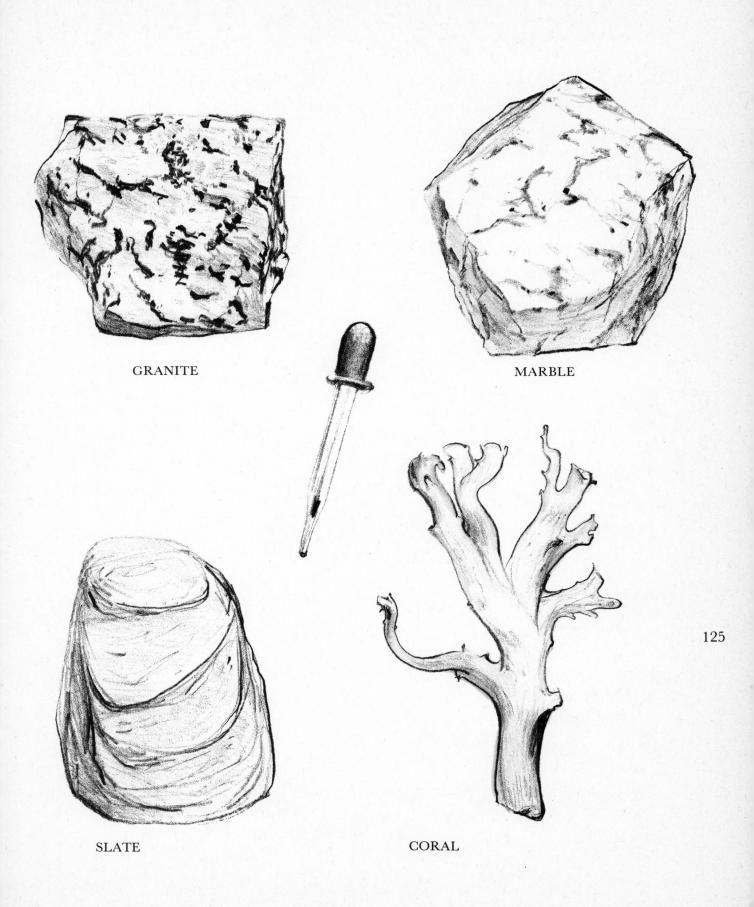

GRANITE

MARBLE

SLATE

CORAL

125

10. How can I make butter?

Butter is made from the cream after it has been separated from whole milk. You then may make some butter by putting about ¼ cup of whipping cream in a pint fruit jar. Drop into the cream a few drops of lactic acid. The lactic acid will cause the butter fat to separate from the buttermilk more easily. Put a top on the jar and begin shaking it with a regular movement. After a few minutes you will see little lumps of butter. Shake gently and the little lumps will become one big lump of butter. The buttermilk can then be poured off of the butter. You will probably wish to salt the butter before it is eaten.

Now you know that:

Oxygen and iron combine to make rust.

When a candle burns it is really gas that is burning.

When vinegar and soda are combined carbon dioxide
is formed.

Limewater is a test for carbon dioxide.

Iodine is a test for starch.

The spot test is a test for fats.

Potatoes have much water in them.

Litmus paper can be used as a test for acids.

Hydrochloric acid can be used to test for lime in rocks.

PLANTS

1. What is inside of a seed?

You will need at least six bean seeds to do this experiment.

Drop three bean seeds in fresh, clear, cool water and let them stand. Three or four hours later examine the seeds. Compare the ones in water to the ones which were not in water. The ones in water are bigger and the seed coat may be wrinkled and broken. Now with your thumb and front finger open the seed.

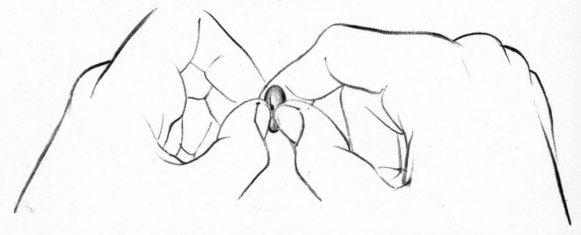

On the inside you will find something which looks like this:

130

The parts which you see are the baby plant or embryo, as it is called, and the food for the embryo. The two halves in which the food is stored are called the cotyledons.

2. How does water get inside of a seed?

Select six bean seeds whose seed coats appear to have no cracks or openings in them. Examine them carefully. You will notice no marks on them except on one side.

There you will see what appears to be a white scar and a tiny spot at one end of the scar on each of them. Light a candle and let some of the wax drip on the scar and on the tiny spot at the end of it.   Do this to all six of them. Now select six more bean seeds which seem to have no cracks or openings in the coat. Put all twelve of these seeds in water and let stand overnight. Examine them in the morning. The ones with the wax on them are likely to look as they did when they were put in the water. The other six are likely to look swollen and some of them may have wrinkled and split seed coats.

131

Water enters the bean seed through a little opening near the white scar. The opening was the spot you saw. In six of them you filled it with wax so that the water could not get in unless there were other openings in the coat which you did not see. The opening is called the microphyle.

3. *What happens when a seed begins to grow?*

To do an experiment to answer this question you will need: a glass funnel, paper toweling, a pint milk bottle, three bean seeds, sand, and some water.

Put the seeds in water and let stand for several hours or overnight. Place the funnel in the milk bottle. Fold the paper toweling in half like this and now fold it again like this. Put it in the funnel and cut it to fit.

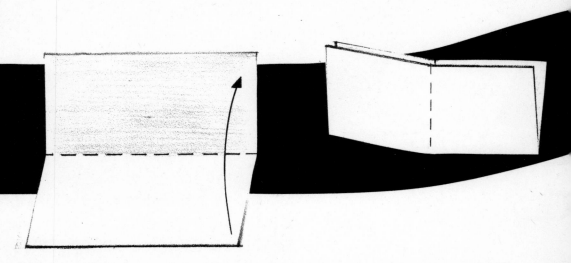

Pour sand into the paper until it is about half full. Put the three seeds which were soaked in water between the glass and the paper in three different places.

Add more sand until it comes almost to the top of the paper. Pour water on the sand until it is wet and the paper soaked. Some of the water will run through into the milk bottle. Put this in a warm light place and water it each day. Watch carefully to see what happens. You will probably first notice a tiny root coming out of the seed.

Then you will see a little loop which will be the stem. After a few days the loop will straighten up and bring up with it the two parts of the bean seed. The two cotyledons become like leaves for the little plant.

132

4. Do all seeds look alike when they begin to grow?

For this experiment you will need; three bean seeds, three corn seeds, three radish seeds, a powder funnel, paper toweling, some sand, a pint milk bottle.

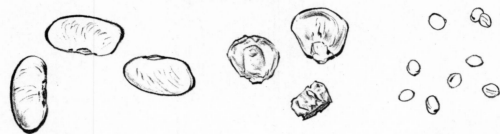

Put the seeds in water to soak for 3 or 4 hours. Place the funnel in the milk bottle and put the paper in it just as you did in experiment Number 3. Now put in the sand. Place the seeds in between the paper and the glass.

Set the experiment in a suitable place and watch them begin to grow. You know what to expect the beans to look like as they grow. You must watch the corn and radish seeds to see whether they look the same. The corn will be quite different. Instead of a loop coming up it sends up a sharp green point. The point is really folded leaves. The corn seed never comes up into the air as the bean seed did. The radish looked more like the bean but it was much smaller. The bean and radish seeds are called dicotyledons because they have two parts to the seed. The corn seeds are called monocotyledons because they only have one part to the seed.

Now you know that not all seeds look alike as they begin to grow.

134

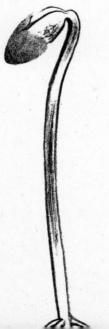

5. Will seeds germinate in dark places?

To do an experiment to answer this question you will need; 2 finger bowls, 2 pieces of blotter paper, at least 30 radish seeds, some Saran Wrap or two pieces of glass, and water.

In each bowl place a piece of blotter paper which has been cut to fit the bowl. Pour a little water into each of the bowls. When the blotter paper is soaked with water pour off the rest of the water. Put seeds on the wet blotter papers. Now cover the bowls with Saran Wrap or with glass.

One of the bowls should be placed in a warm dark place. The other bowl should be placed in an equally warm but light place.

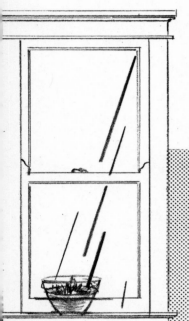

Look at the seeds each day. In a few days a seed will crack and a plant will begin to grow just as you saw happen in the last experiment. There will be a velvety covering of fine roothairs on the root. The seeds in both the light and dark places should begin to grow or germinate as we call it.

If none of the seeds grow we can think that the seeds were not good because we have already found out that seeds treated this way will germinate in the light. The last experiment showed us that seeds will germinate in light places.

6. What happens if the roots of a plant get started growing up instead of down?

Find two pieces of glass four or five inches square. Cut a piece of blotting paper the same size of the glass. Lay the blotting paper on one of the pieces of glass and pour water on it. After the paper is soaked with water drain off the rest of the water. Now sprinkle a few radish seeds on the blotting paper. Place the other glass over them and fasten the edges of the glass together with tape at each side.

Now stand the glass up in a shallow pan of water and fix a support for it so that it will stay that way. The radish seeds will begin to grow. Now turn the glass around so that the roots will point up instead of down and the tops point down instead of up. Notice what happens. After a time the roots will begin to turn around and point down again. You probably noticed that the tops have turned around too. They have begun to point up again. There is something inside of plants which causes the tops to grow toward the light and the roots to grow in the direction from which the gravity pulls. If roots get started growing up instead of down they turn around and go down.

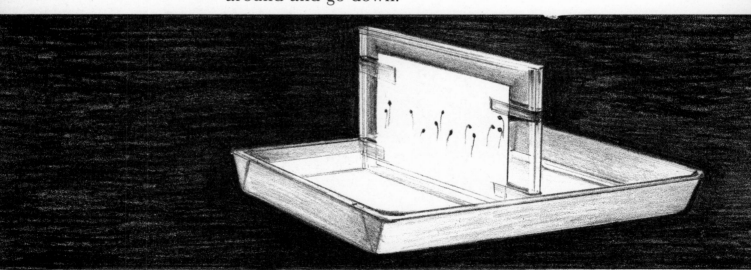

7. *Will green leaves grow from bulbs which have been in the dark?*

Get six Narcissus bulbs. Plant three of them in pebbles or shells. Plant the other three in another dish in the same way.

Place both containers in a dark place and water them well. Check them each day to see if they need more water and to see what is happening to them.
You will notice that they start to grow but that the leaves are yellow instead of green. When the leaves are about six inches high move one of the containers out into the light and leave the other in the dark. Compare them each day.

The one which is moved to the light begins to get green but the other one stays yellow. Now move the second one out into the light and see what happens to it. It will begin to get green, too. The leaves will get green only if they have sunlight.

137

8. *How does water get up to the leaves of a plant?*

Find two glasses about five-inches high. Put water in each of them. Color the water in one of them red and the water in the other blue with food coloring. Set them close side by side. Get a stick of celery which is nine or ten inches long.

Cut the stick of celery about one-half way up. Put one side in one glass of colored water and the other half in the other glass of colored water. Let this stand for about two hours. Notice what has happened to the color of the celery. The red color has gone up on one side and the blue color has gone up the other side. Take the celery out of the water and dry it. Now cut across the celery stalk. You will notice spots of color which shows where the colored water went up the stem. These are the water tubes in the stem. Water goes up to the leaves through the water tubes.

138

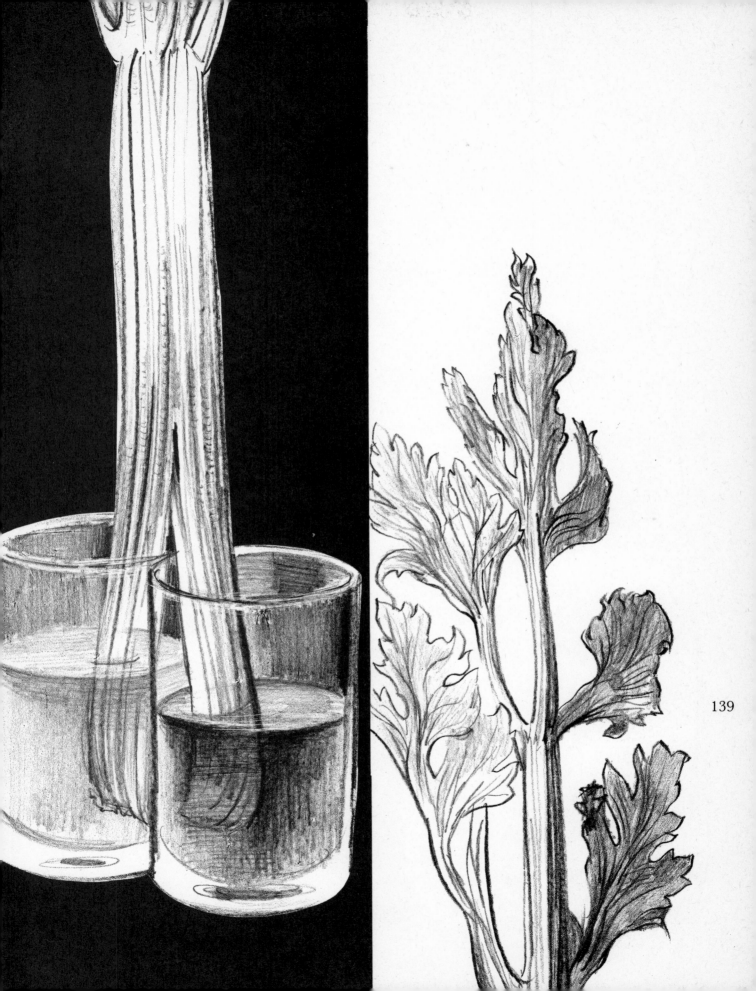

139

9. *What do yeast plants need in order to become active?*

140

Get a package of dry yeast. The yeast looks like dry powder. In this dry powder are many little inactive plants. Put a teaspoonful of this yeast in a cup. Put another teaspoonful of yeast in another cup and the same amount in a third cup.

In two of these cups add mildly warm water until the cup is about half full. To one of these cups of water and yeast add one teaspoonful of sugar.

Set all three cups aside for about one-half hour. Examine to see what has happened. You will see nothing has happened to the dry yeast. The water and yeast alone has no evidence of action. The third cup—the one with the water, yeast and sugar shows much action. There are many bubbles. The sugar is food for the yeast plants. As the yeast plants grow and form more yeast plants they give off carbon dioxide and alcohol. The bubbles you see are bubbles of carbon dioxide.

10. In what kind of place should we expect mold to grow?

Get four dishes which are fairly deep. Place one-half slice of fresh bread in each of them. Cover two of the dishes with pieces of glass.

Put two of the dishes—one with glass and one without glass—in a warm dark place. Put the other two dishes in a cold place. After about three days look at the pieces of bread. See whether there was any mold on any of it. If there was no mold put it back and wait another day or more if necessary. If mold appears it will most likely be on the bread which was covered with glass and was put in the warm dark place. Mold grows best where there is not much fresh air, where it is warm and where it is dark.

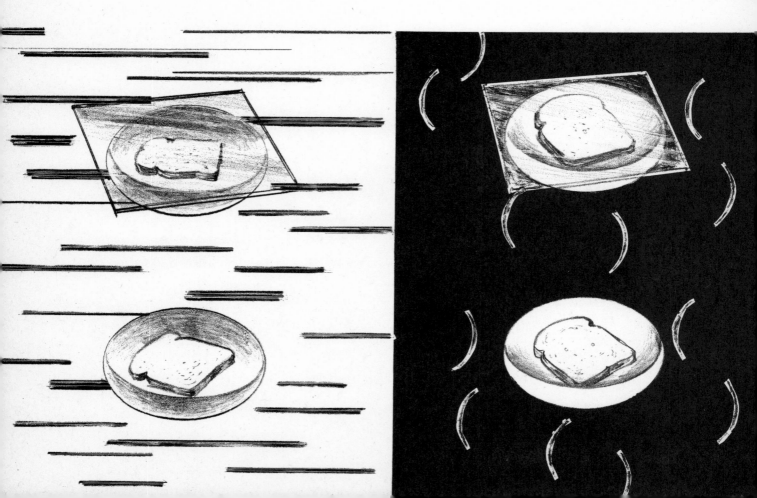

11. Can plants be raised from stems?

Get a philodendron plant which has several branches. Cut off about six inches of one of the branches. Pull off the leaves near where the stem was cut. Put the branch in water so that the water comes up over the place where the leaves were pulled off. Keep the branch watered and watch for roots to develop. When some of the roots are an inch or more long it is ready to be planted in dirt.

Find a flower pot and put a few shells or pieces of broken flower pot in the bottom. Fill the pot about half full of rich dirt. Hold the roots in the pot and put more dirt in around the plant. Fill the pot almost to the top. Water the dirt. Put dry dirt on top and press down lightly. Set the plant where it will get sunlight and water as it needs it.

There are several kinds of plants which can be raised from stems in much this same way. You might try raising geraniums in this way.

143

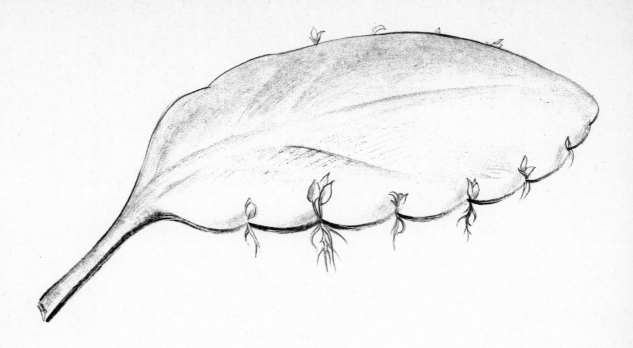

12. *Can plants be raised from leaves?*

Ask at a greenhouse for a leaf of a bryophyllum plant. Lay the leaf in a shallow dish of water. Keep it watered and watch for signs of a tiny plant on the edge of the leaf. There may be one or there may be many.

Prepare a flower pot with good soil as you did the one in experiment Number 11. With a sharp knife cut the new little plant away from the leaf as you see in the picture. Put the new little plant on the top of the soil and press around it lightly.

African violets can be started from their leaves too. Their leaves can be put in water and rooted just as the stems were rooted in experiment Number 11.

Now you know that:

A seed contains an embryo and food for the embryo.

Water goes into the seed through the little opening on one side.

Not all seeds look alike when they begin to grow.

Seeds will germinate in dark places.

Seeds will germinate in light places.

Roots grow downward and leaf parts grow upward.

Leaves are green when they grow in the sunlight.

Water moves upward in the stems of plants.

Sugar is food for yeast plants.

Molds grow best where it is warm and dark and there is not much fresh air.

Plants can be raised from stems.

Plants can be raised from leaves.

MORE EXPERIMENTS

147

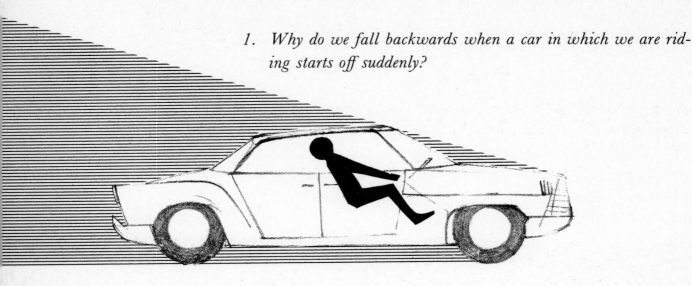

1. Why do we fall backwards when a car in which we are riding starts off suddenly?

Perhaps this experiment will help us answer this question. Place a card on a water glass and put a penny on the center of the card. Now with your finger push the card off of the glass. The penny went off with the card. Put the card and the penny on the glass again. This time shoot the card off with your thumb and finger.

The penny will fall into the glass. The card went off of the glass so fast that the penny did not have a chance to get started. The penny could not get started because of inertia. When any thing is still it tends to stay still unless something starts it moving.

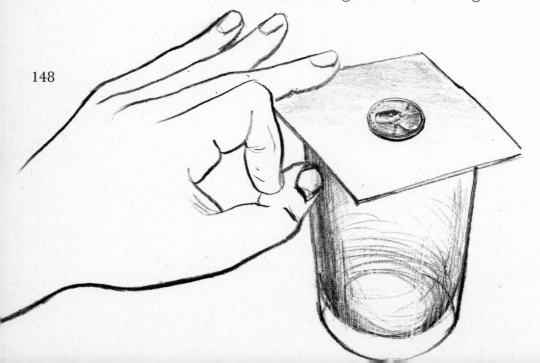

2. When a car stops suddenly why do we go forward?

Place three or four books stacked one on top of the other on top of your hand. Walk forward fast with the books. Stop suddenly. Do this experiment several times. The books slide forward off of your hand. You can feel them slide. They do this for the same reason that you go forward when the car stops. Things which are moving have a tendency to keep moving in that direction unless something stops them. This is because of inertia.

3. Why are there more pebbles some places than others?

Use a tall glass jar. Put in the jar about an inch of sand. On top of the sand put about an inch of small pebbles and on top of the pebbles about the same amount of dirt. Now fill the jar about three-fourths full of water and shake the jar until every thing in it is very well mixed. Stand the jar aside for over night. The next day it will look quite different than it did when you left it. You will notice that the water is almost clear. You will notice, too, that almost all of the pebbles are near the bottom with the sand among them and on top of them. On top of the sand and pebbles is a fine layer of dirt. The pebbles fall first because they are heavier. The dirt falls last because it is lighter. It takes a long time for all of the dirt to settle down. When rivers carry a heavy load of gravel, sand and mud they drop the gravel first then the sand and at last the mud. They drop the gravel, sand and mud when the river slows down and stops flowing so fast. This is one reason that there are more pebbles some places than others.

4. How is the water which is down in the soil useful to plants?

Cut a blotter into several pieces about one-inch wide and four-inches long. Fill a glass almost full of water. Draw a pencil line one-half inch from one end on each of the pieces of blotter paper.

Put one of the blotter papers in the water so that the top of the water in the glass touches the pencil line. Hold it there for one-half minute. Do the same thing with another piece of blotter paper, and another, and another, etc. Lay the blotter papers side by side on the table.

In each of them the water came up. It came up about the same distance too. The paper is many tiny particles pressed together. The water moved around one particle and then on to another and another until it had climbed up in the blotter paper. You might try holding one paper in the water to find out how far the water would climb.

150

5. *Why is it important to hoe gardens even though they may not be weedy?*

Get a piece of bread and a piece of cracker about the same size. Place them in a dish about one-fourth inch apart. Drop a few drops of colored water between them and see what happens. Do this several times and notice whether the same thing happened. You probably noticed that the colored water traveled through the bread much faster than through the cracker. The bread was more porous—it had more spaces in it than the cracker had. If we hoe our gardens and keep the soil soft and porous around the plants more water will rise in the soil and be useful to the plant.

6. *How many paper clips can be put in a glass full of water?
This question is rather like a puzzle—you may be surprised
at the answer.*

Fill a glass full of water. Begin one after another
putting in paper clips. Put each one in—end first and
carefully. Be sure to count them. You may wish to pre-
dict how many you think you can put in before you start.
If you predicted ten you missed it a long way because
you may be able to put in more than a hundred. There
is a very thin skin or film over the water which makes it
possible for the water to "pile up."

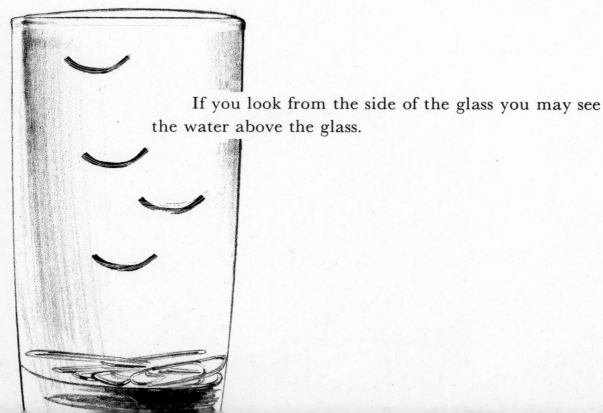

If you look from the side of the glass you may see
the water above the glass.

7. *In the picture you see a little girl with a butterfly on her finger. You are sure it is not a real butterfly and you are probably wondering—*

How does she get the paper butterfly to stay on her finger?

At the bottom of this page is the outline of a paper butterfly. Cut a butterfly this shape from a very heavy paper or a light weight cardboard. Color it as you wish. On the underside of each front wing tip tape a penny. Scotch tape will do. Now try balancing the butterfly on your finger. What you have done is put the same amount of weight on each side. Each of the weights are being pulled down by gravity and they pull down on the butterfly wing. This causes the head of the butterfly to press against your finger and balance there.

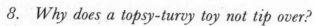

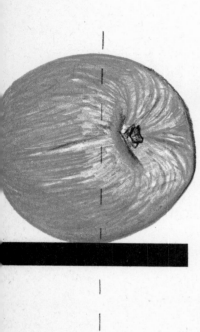

8. Why does a topsy-turvy toy not tip over?

    Get a nice round apple. Cut the apple in two halves. Place each half on the table with the round side down. Try tipping it from one side to the other. You will notice that the apple touches the table at the middle of the half. Now cut each of the half pieces of apple in two pieces. Place each of them on the table with the rounded side down. They also touch the table at the middle of the rounded side.

    The apples touch the table at a point where there is the same amount of apple on each side. The amount of apple on one side balances the amount on the opposite side. This will help you understand why the topsy-turvy toy does not tip over. The point at which the apple touches the table is in line with the center of gravity.

154

Now you know that:

When a thing is still it tends to stay still unless something starts it moving.

Things which are moving have a tendency to continue moving unless something stops them.

Water moves upward in soil.

Water moves upward faster in soil that is porous than in soil that is packed.

There is a thin film or skin over water which makes it possible for water to "pile up."

There are many other experiments which you might do to show these and other important ideas in science. You may find suggestions for doing other experiments in other books. You may plan experiments to show these important ideas and try them out for yourself. Perhaps there are other things which you wonder about. Organize those things which you wonder about into good questions and set out to find the answers. You may read, experiment, or ask questions, but be very sure that you look, listen, think, and work carefully.

INDEX OF EXPERIMENTS

SUGGESTED SOURCES WHERE SCIENCE MATERIALS CAN BE OBTAINED

HOME

Apples
Bottles
Celery
Cloth
Dishes
Dish Pan
Food Coloring
Glass (pieces)
Ice Cubes
Mirrors
Needles (steel)
Paper Clips
Pebbles
Pennies
Pins
Pinwheel
Puffed rice
Sand
Scales
Screw
Seeds
Silk thread
Soda
Towels
Vinegar
Whipping cream
Yeast

DRUGSTORE

Alcohol
Balloons
Blotter Paper
Candles
Iodine
Lactic Acid
Limewater
Marbles
Mirrors

HARDWARE STORE

Balloons
Bells
Bulbs (small light)
Copper wire (cotton covered—bare)
Dry cell
Glass (pieces)
Marbles
Mirrors
Narcissus bulbs
Pulleys
Rods (aluminum, brass, copper, rubber)
Screw
Screw driver
Socket (small to fit the light bulb)
Tops for medicine droppers

CHEMISTRY SET OR SCIENCE KIT

Alcohol
Alcohol Lamp
Balloons
Bells
Candles
Corks
Finger bowls
Flasks
Funnels
Glass tubing
Hydrochloric acid
Iron filings
Litmus paper
Magnets (assorted sizes and shapes)
Prisms
Pulleys
Rods (aluminum, brass, copper, rubber)
Rubber stoppers (one hole, two hole)
Scales
Socket (small to fit the light bulb)
Screw driver
Spring balance
Test tubes
Thermometers
Tops for medicine droppers
Tuning forks